Gilmore Girls

Jenny Penny

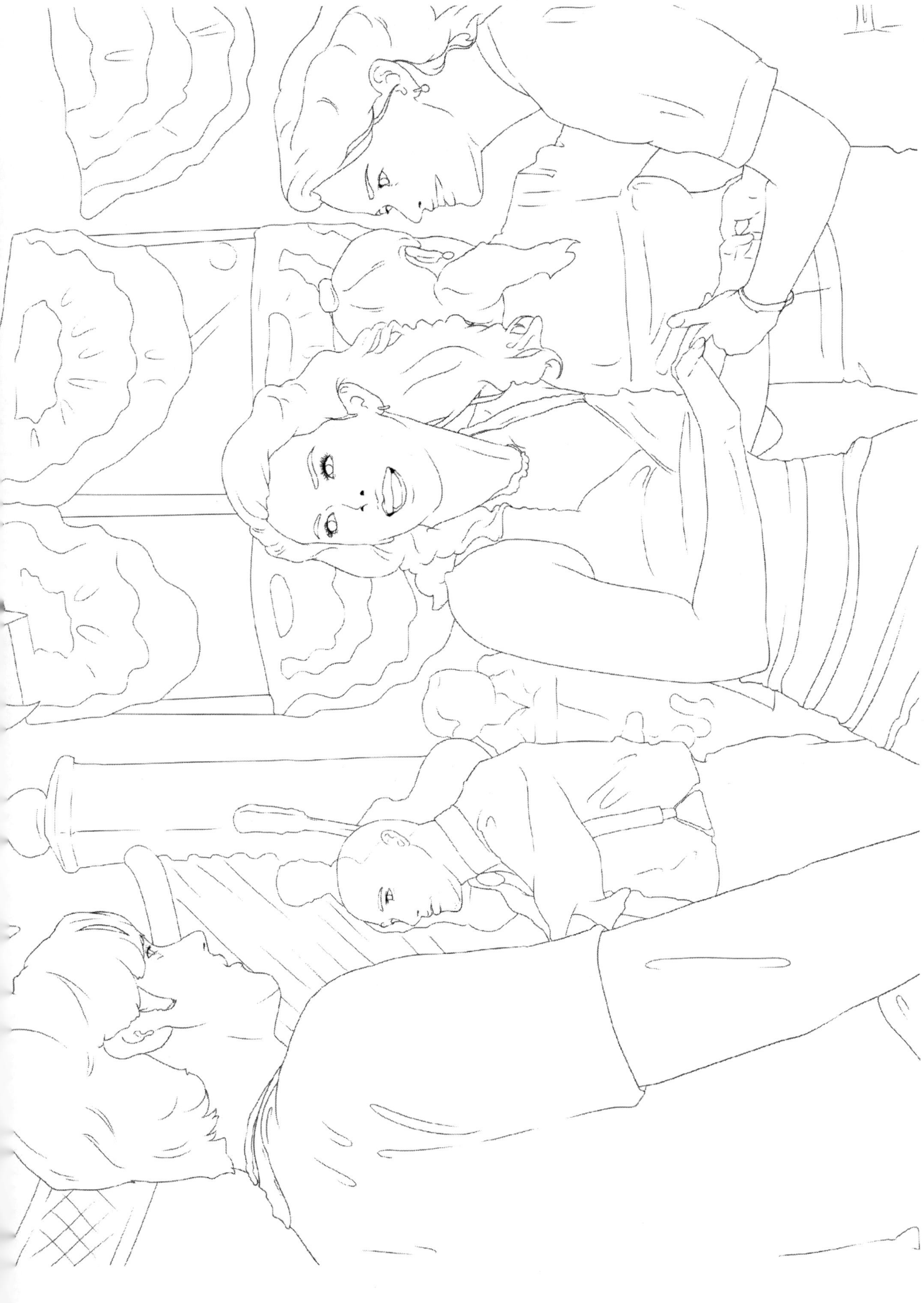

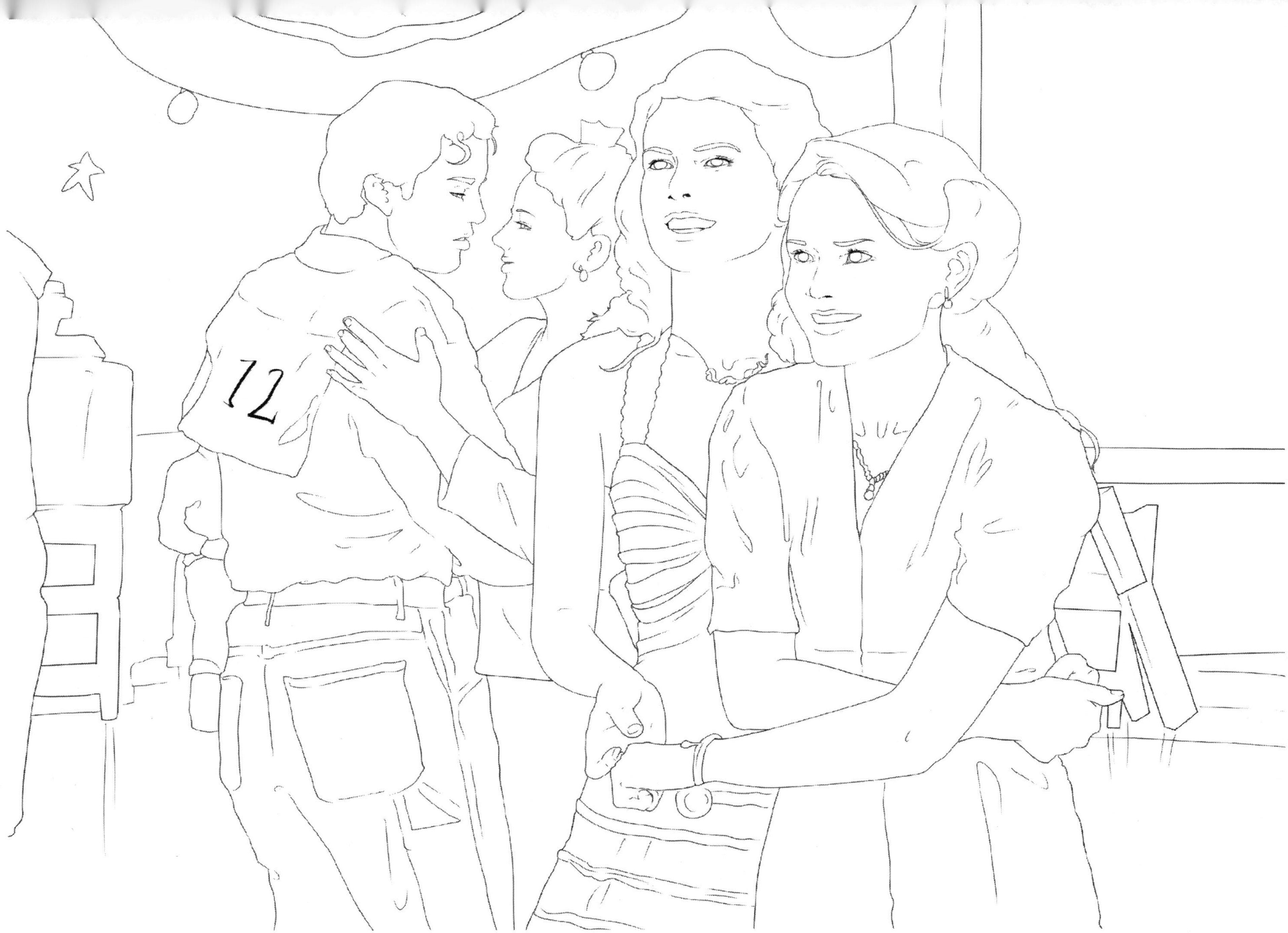
12

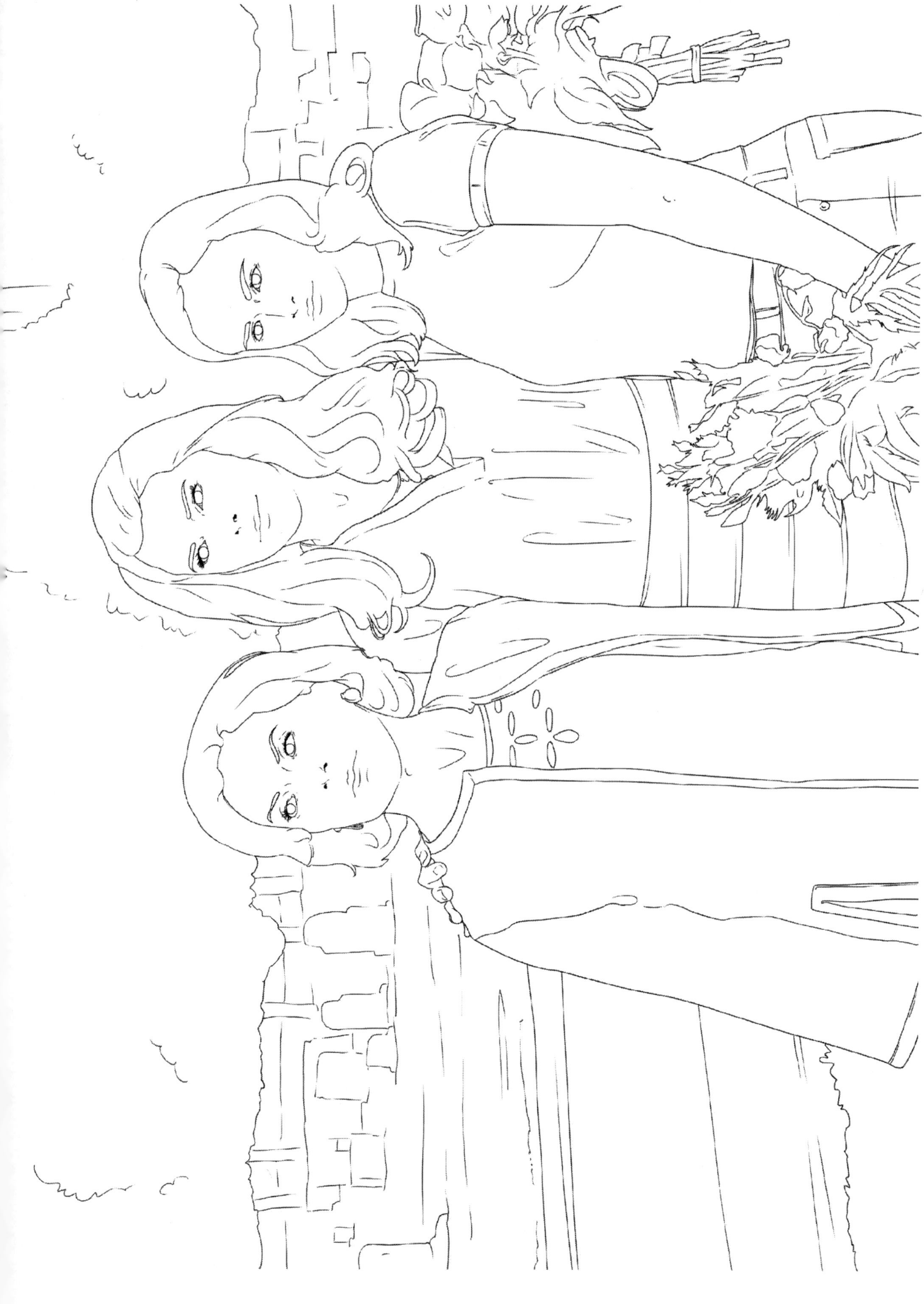

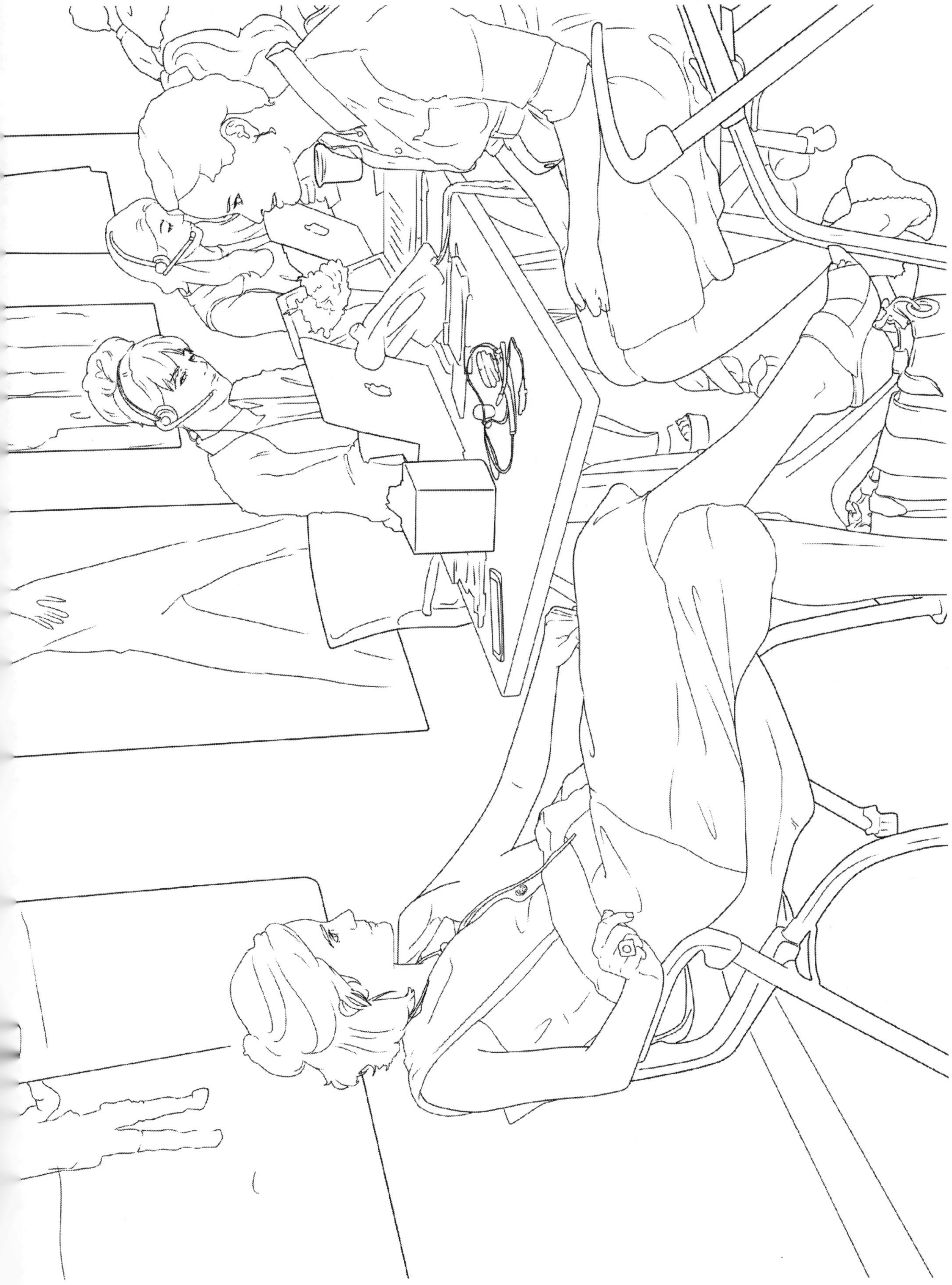

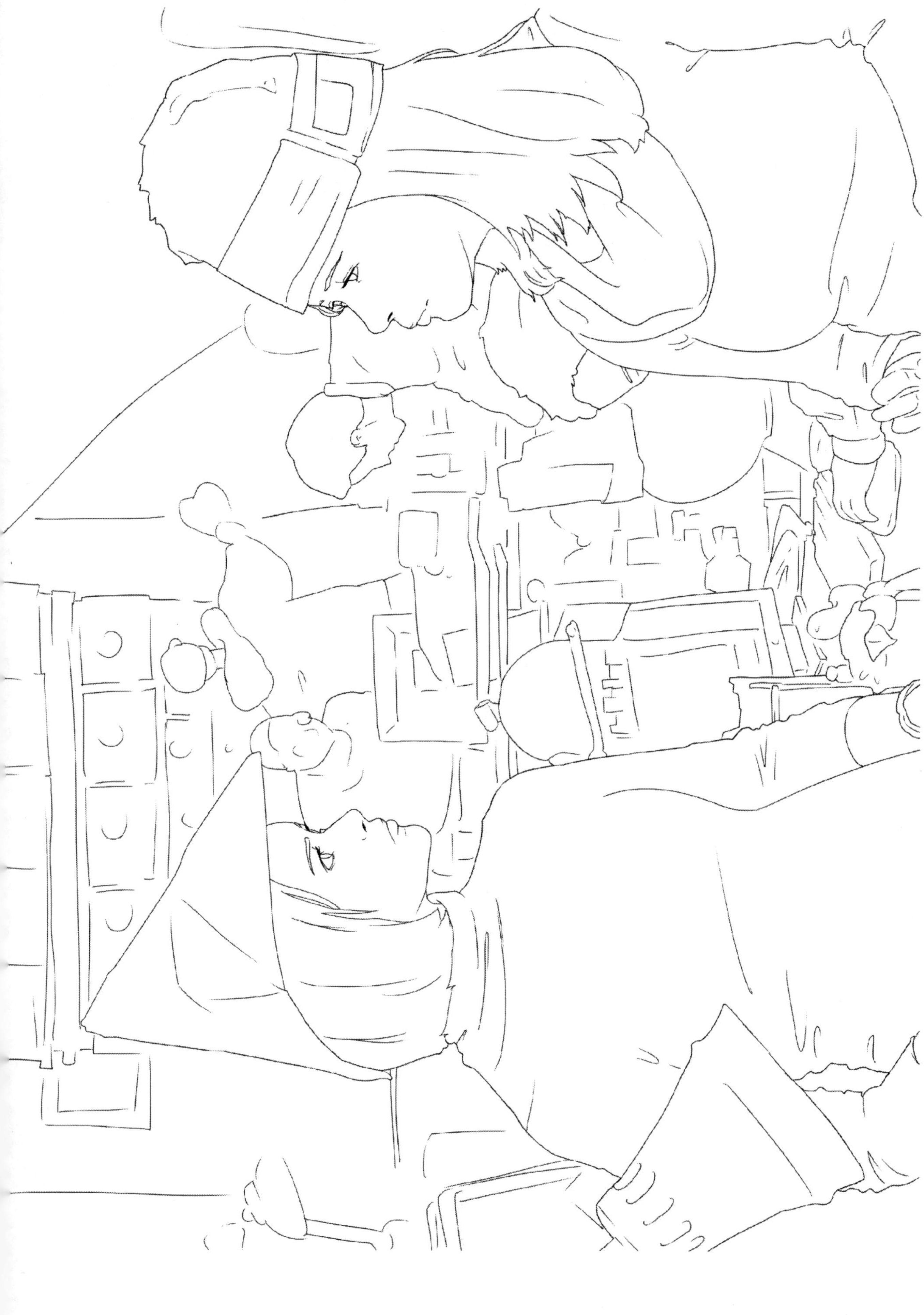

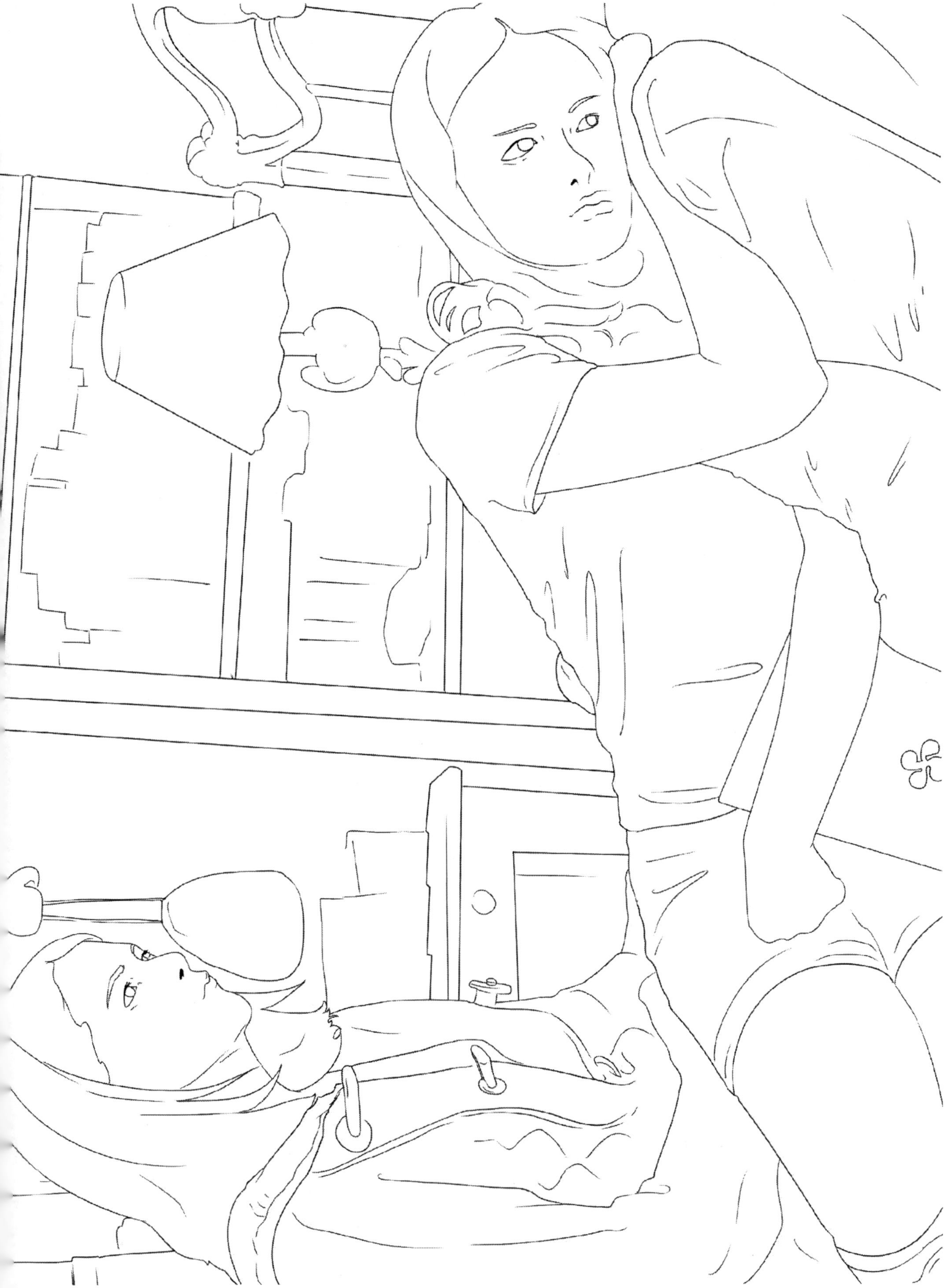

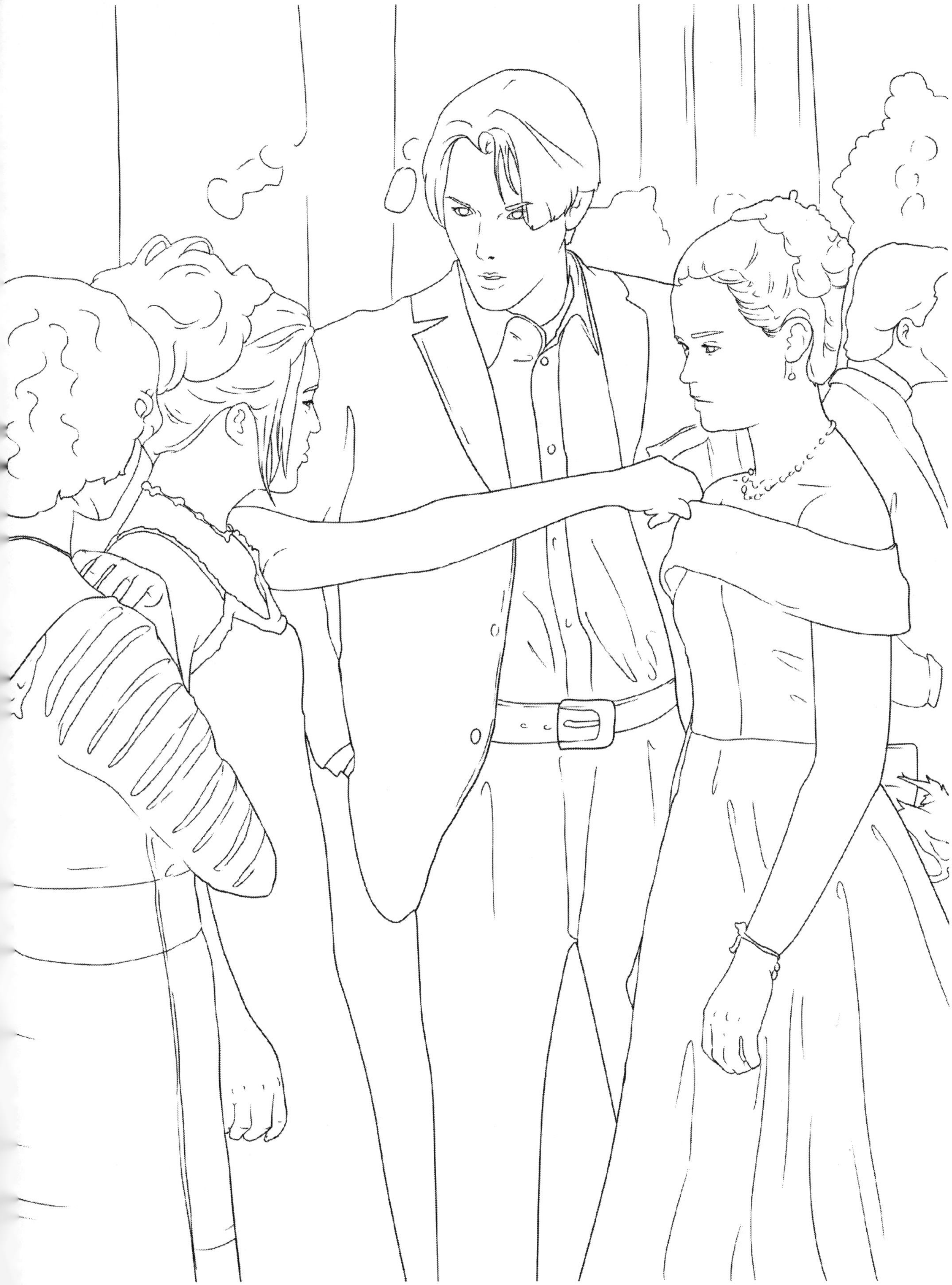

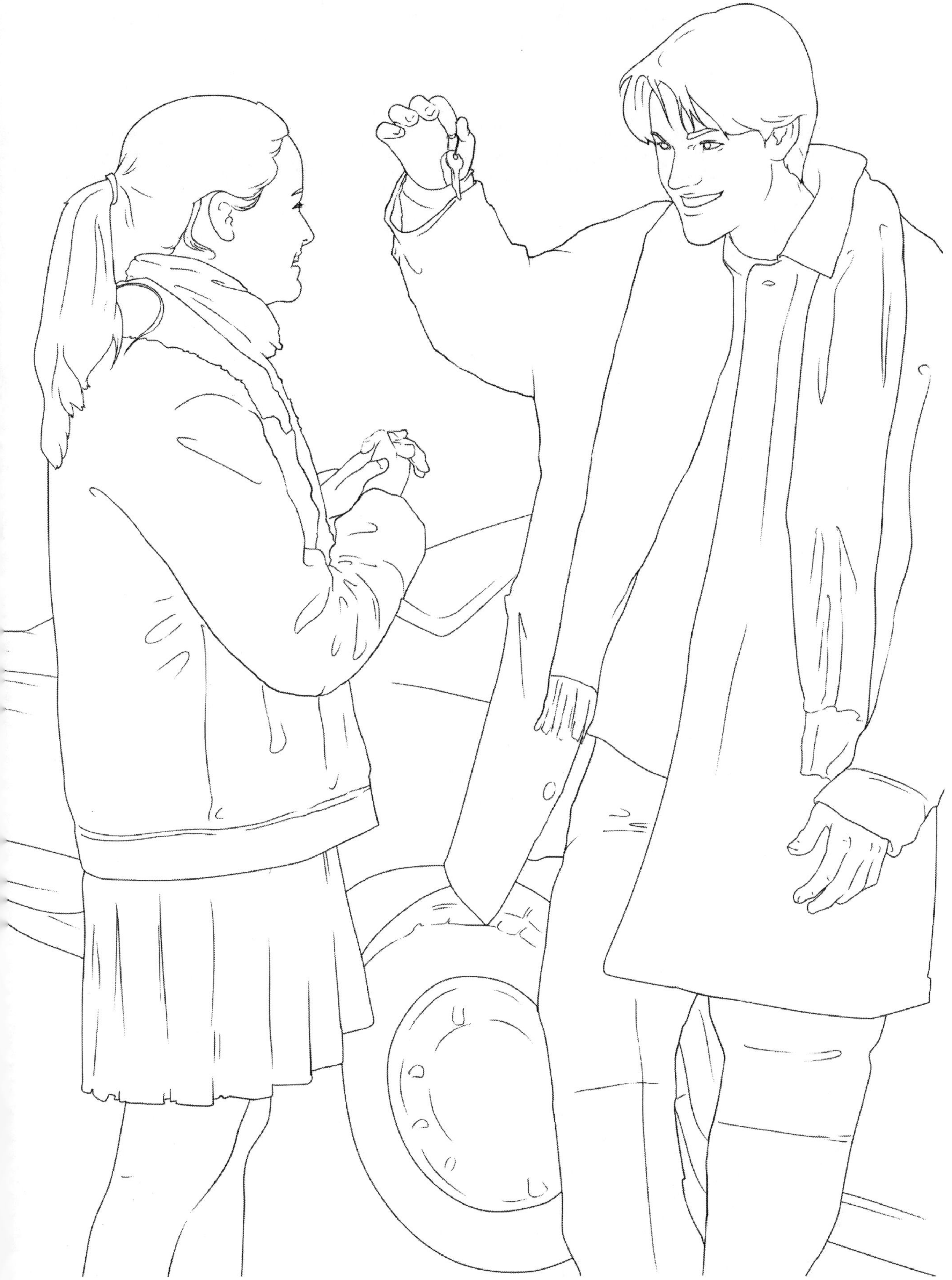

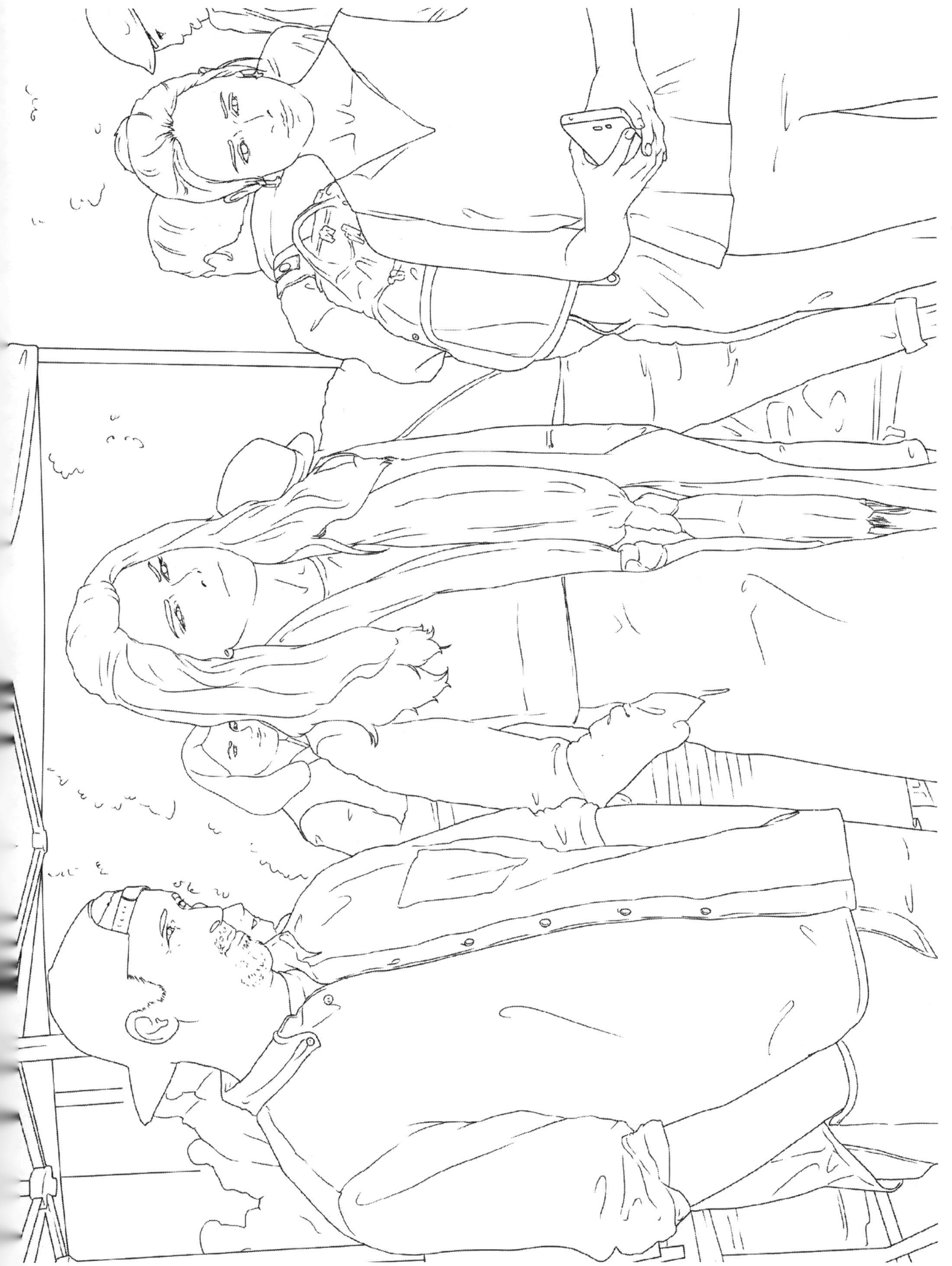

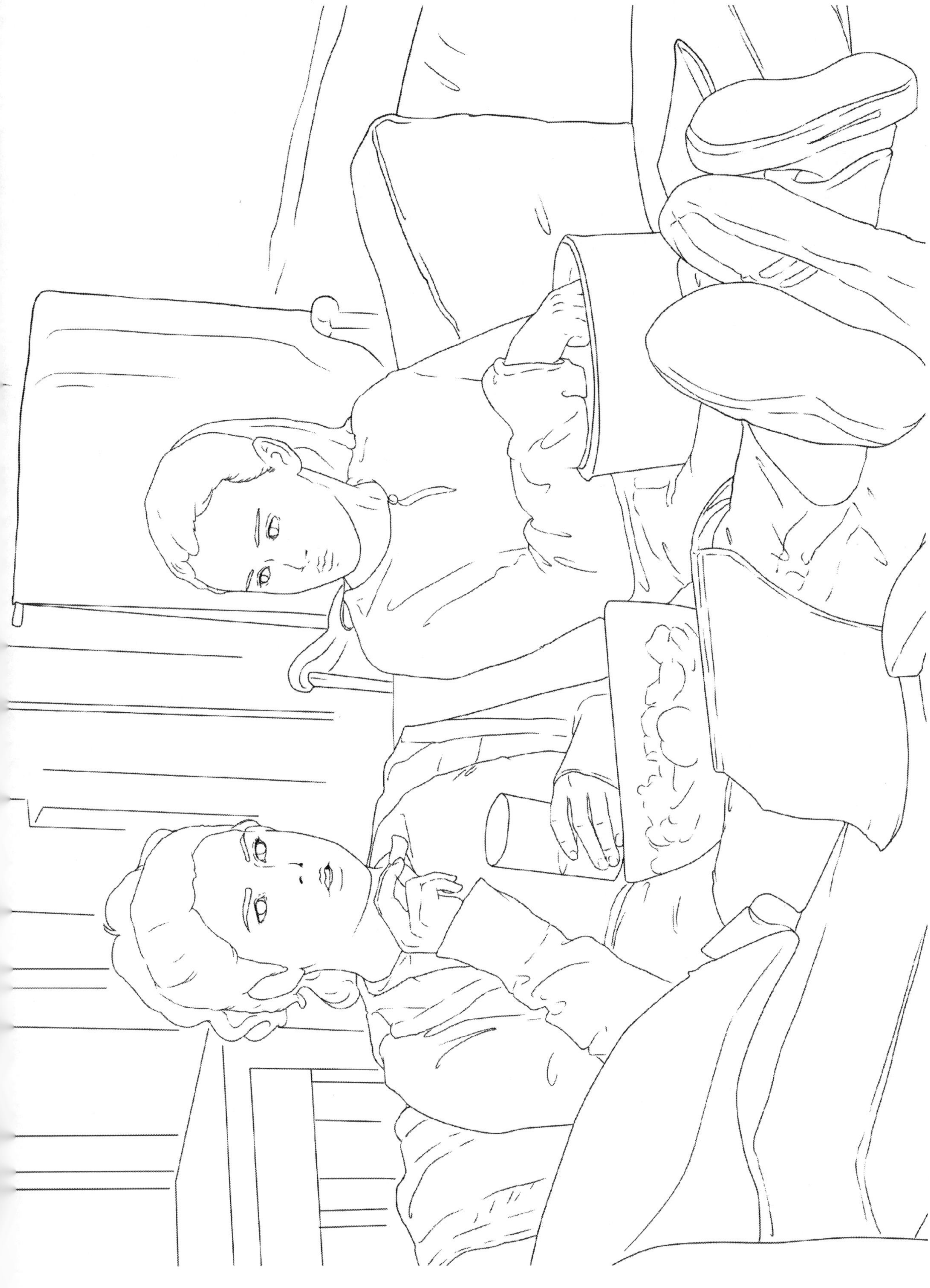

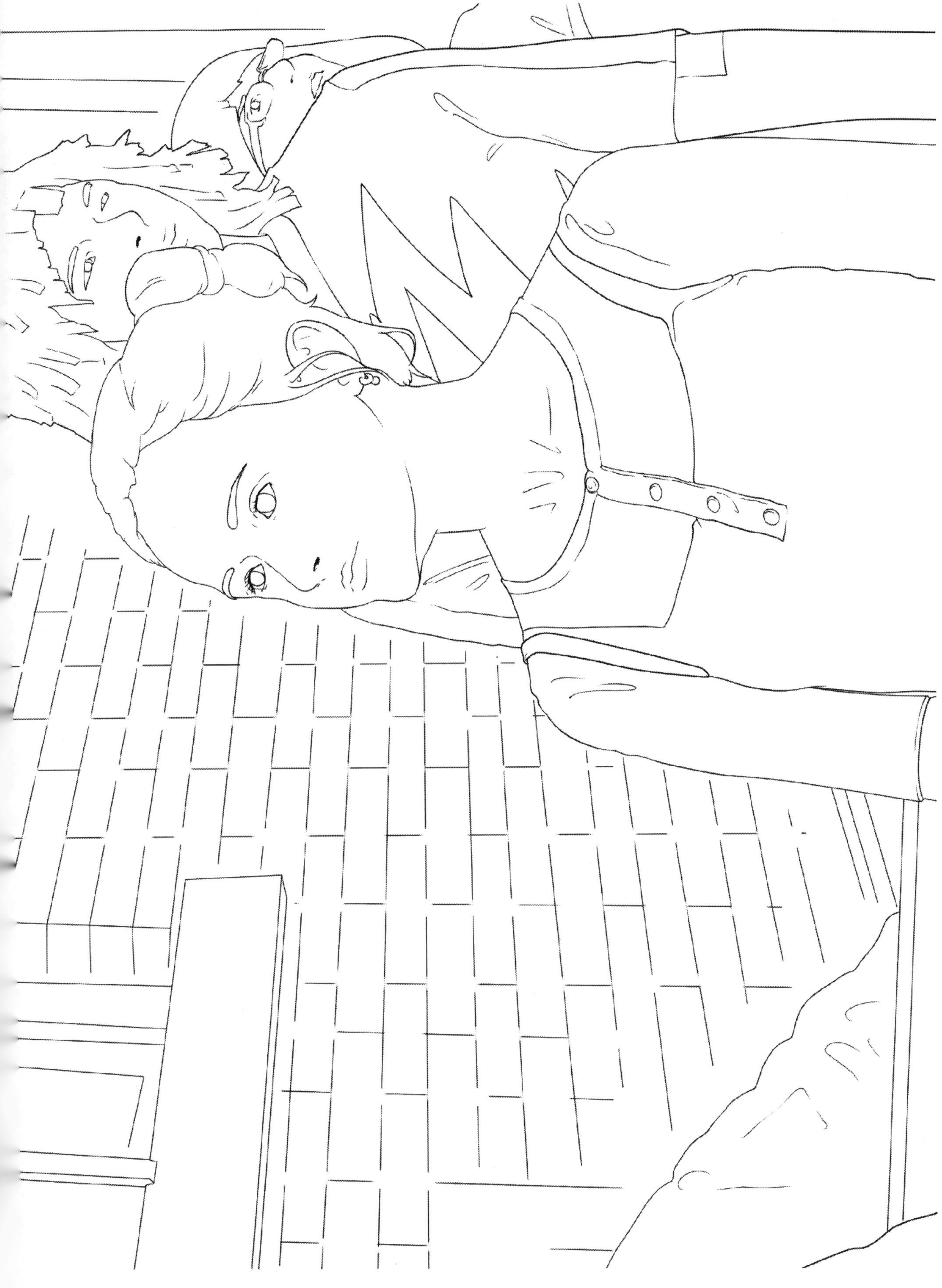

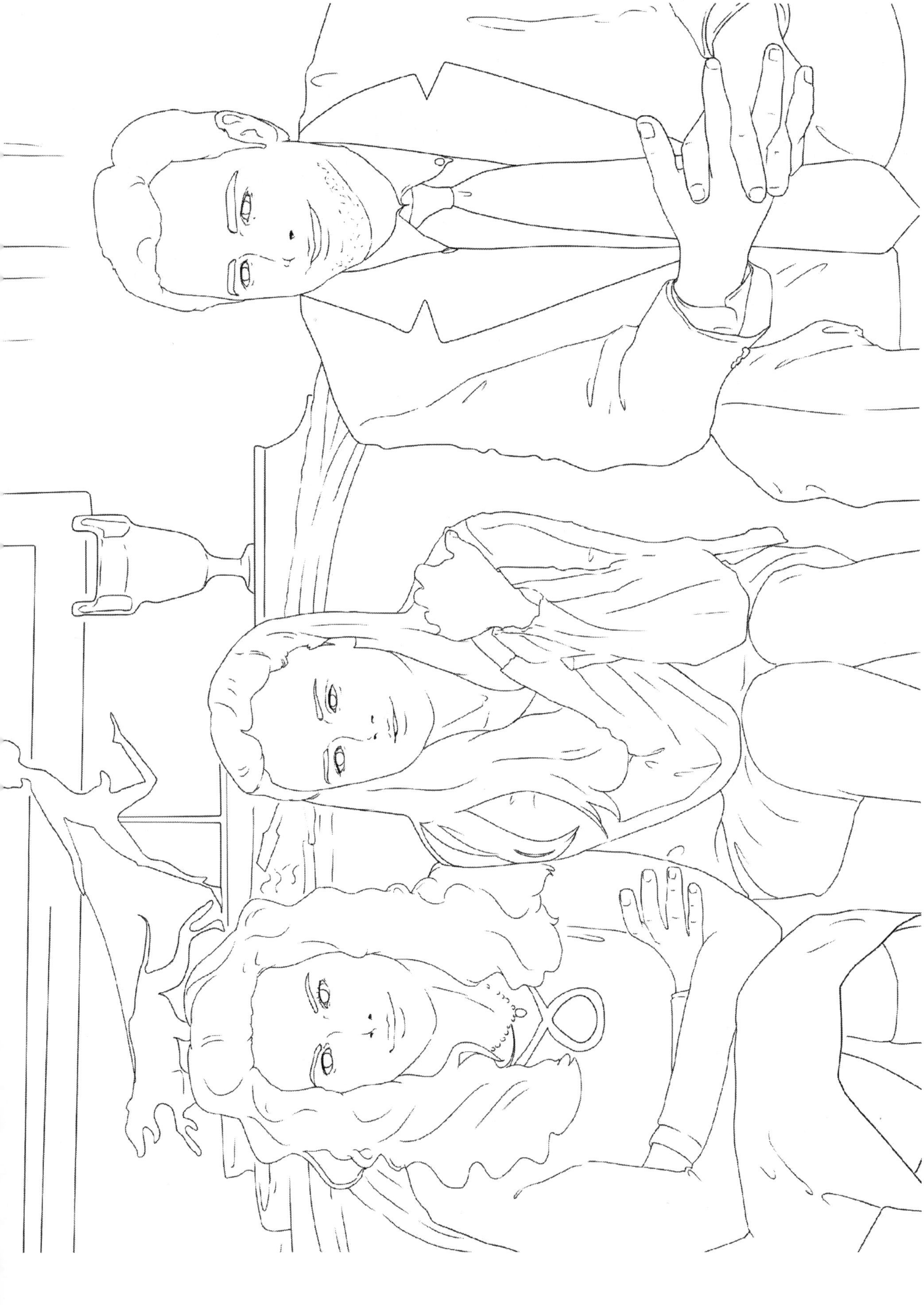

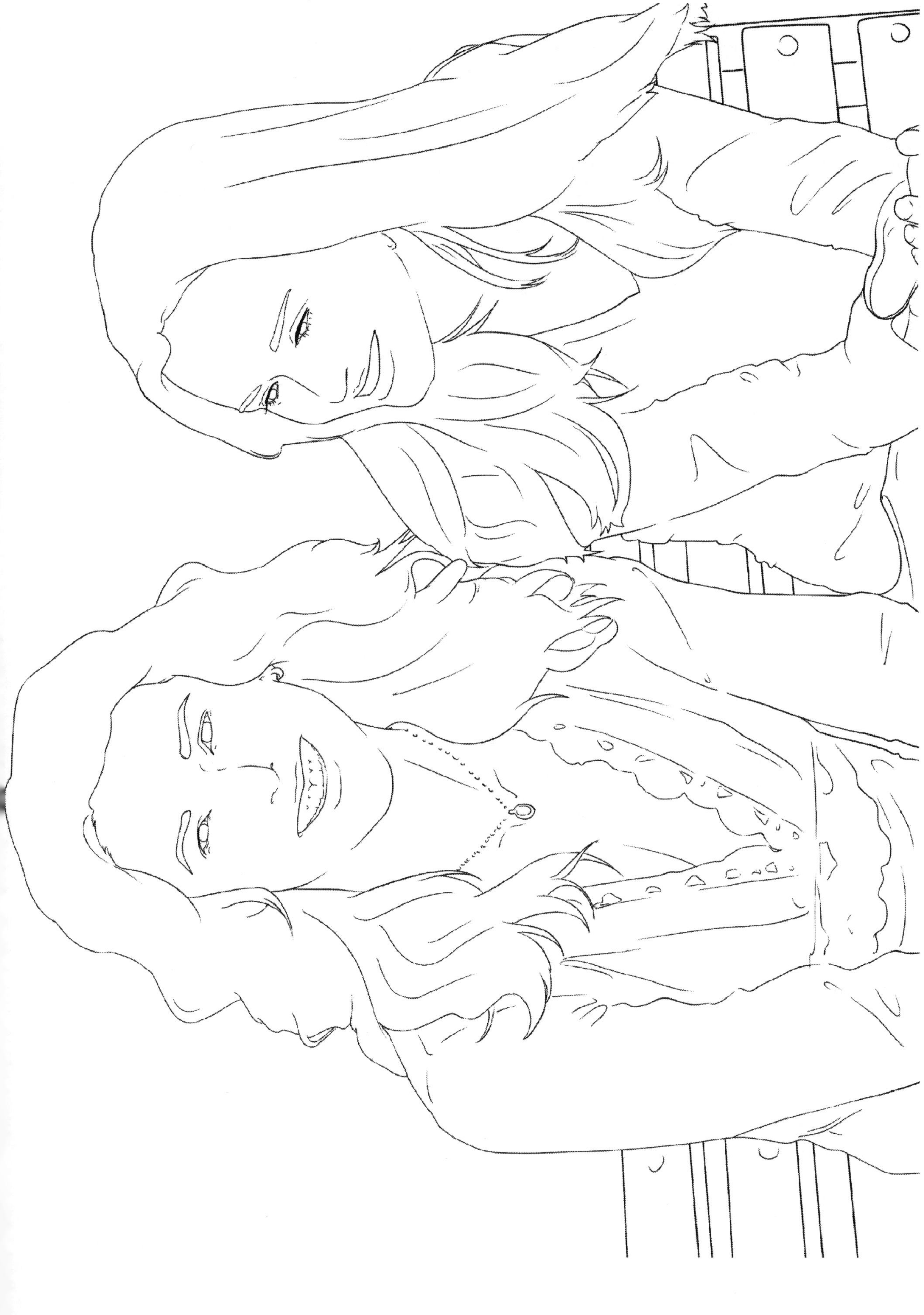

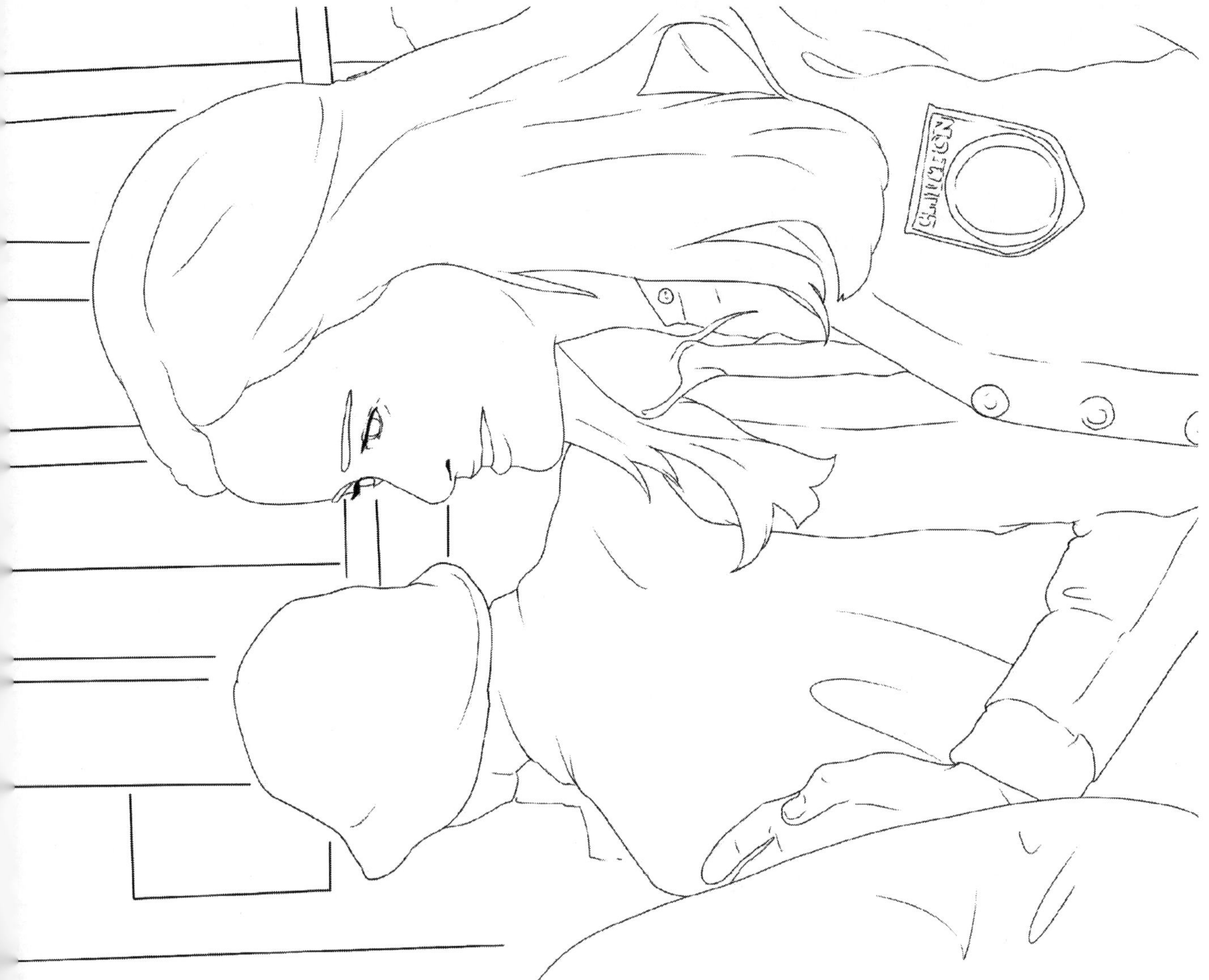

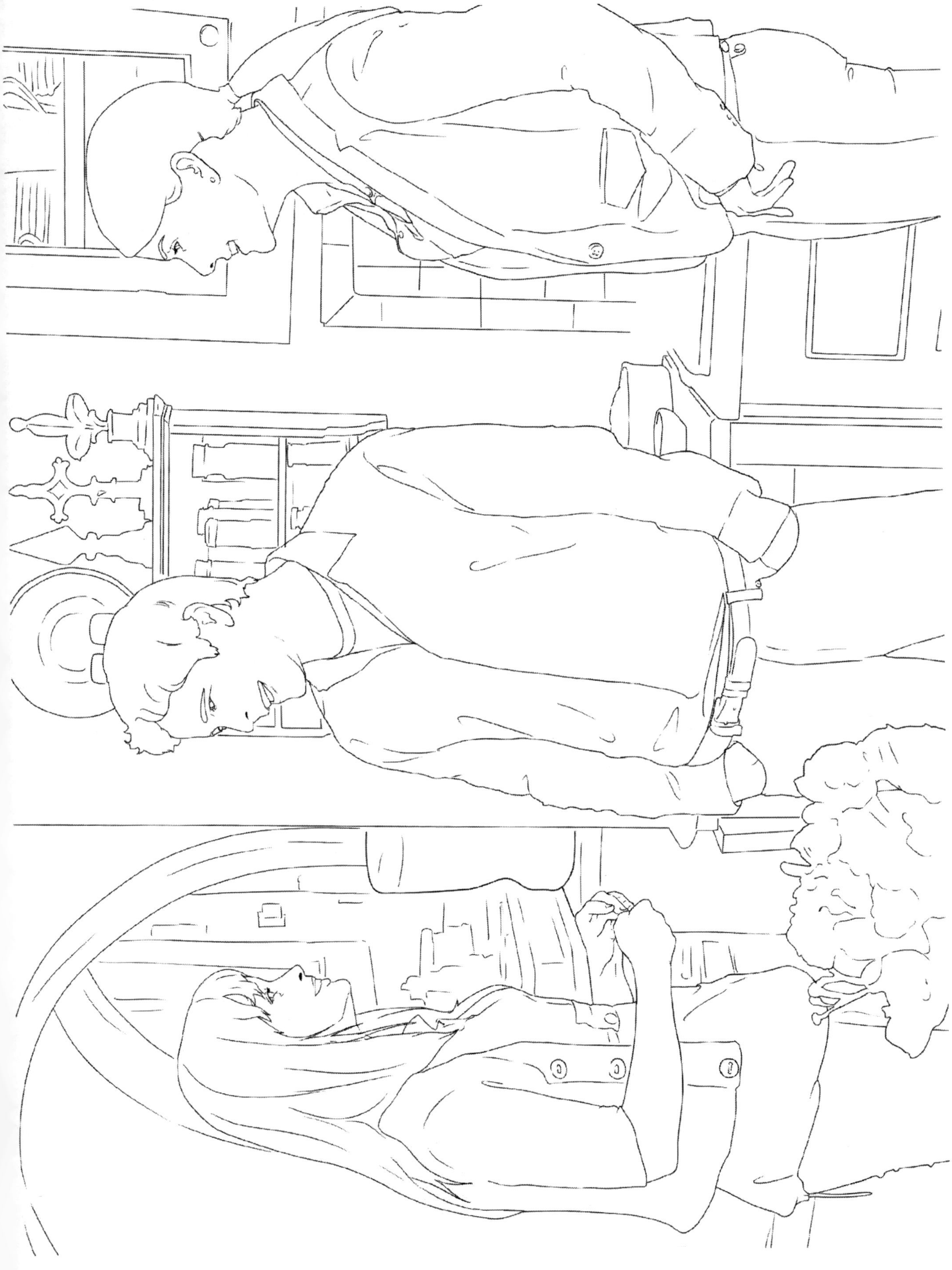

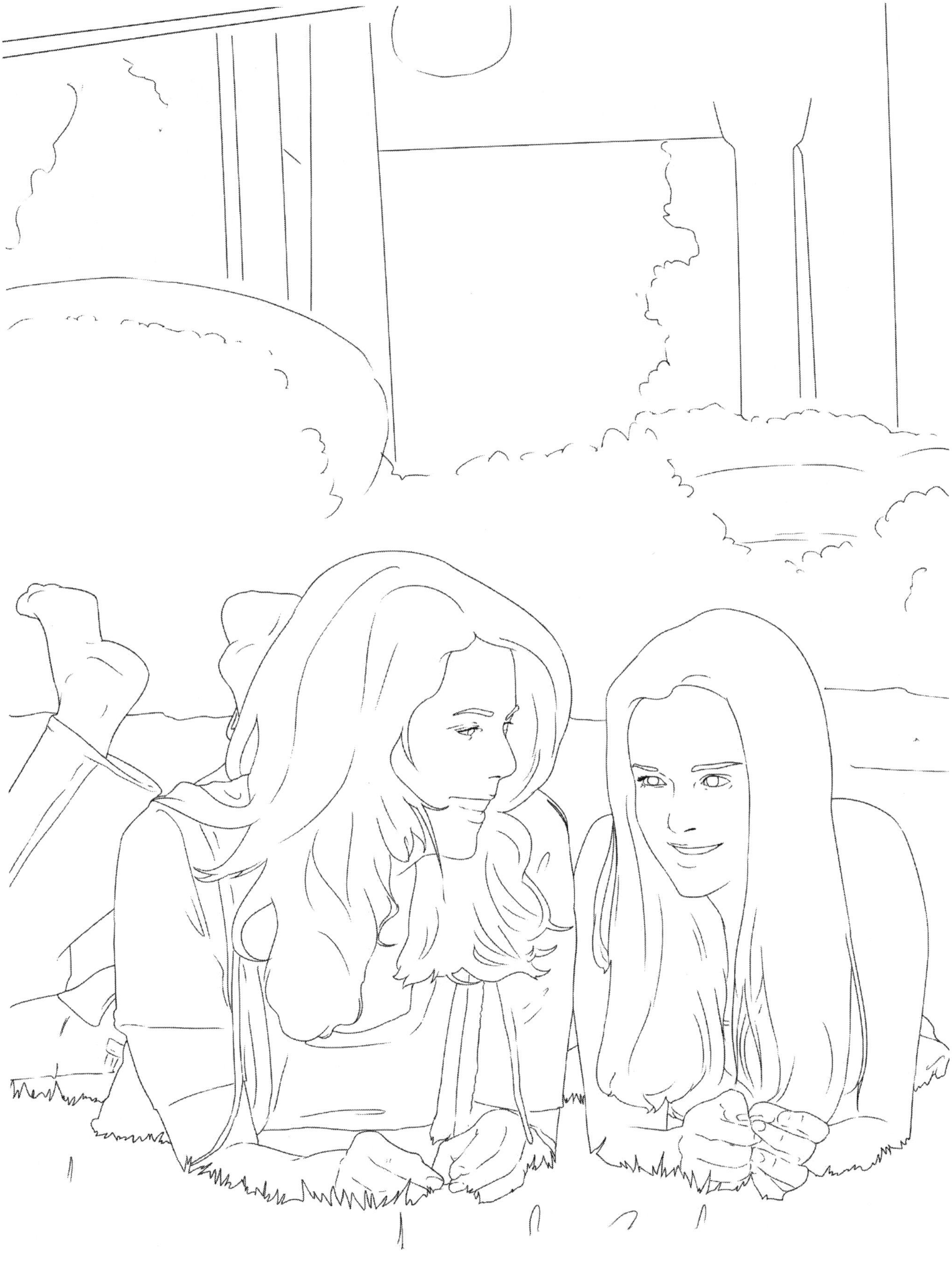

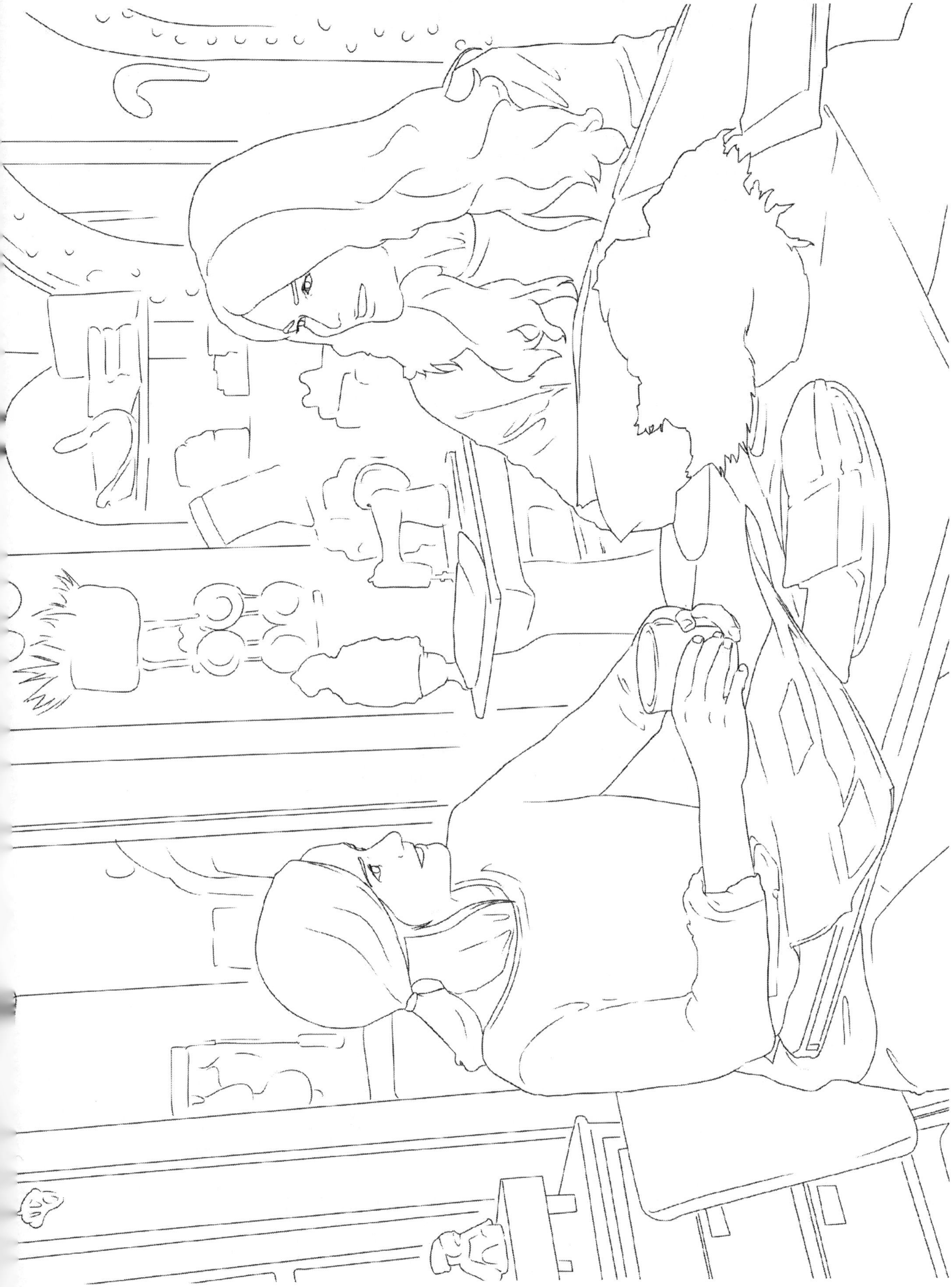

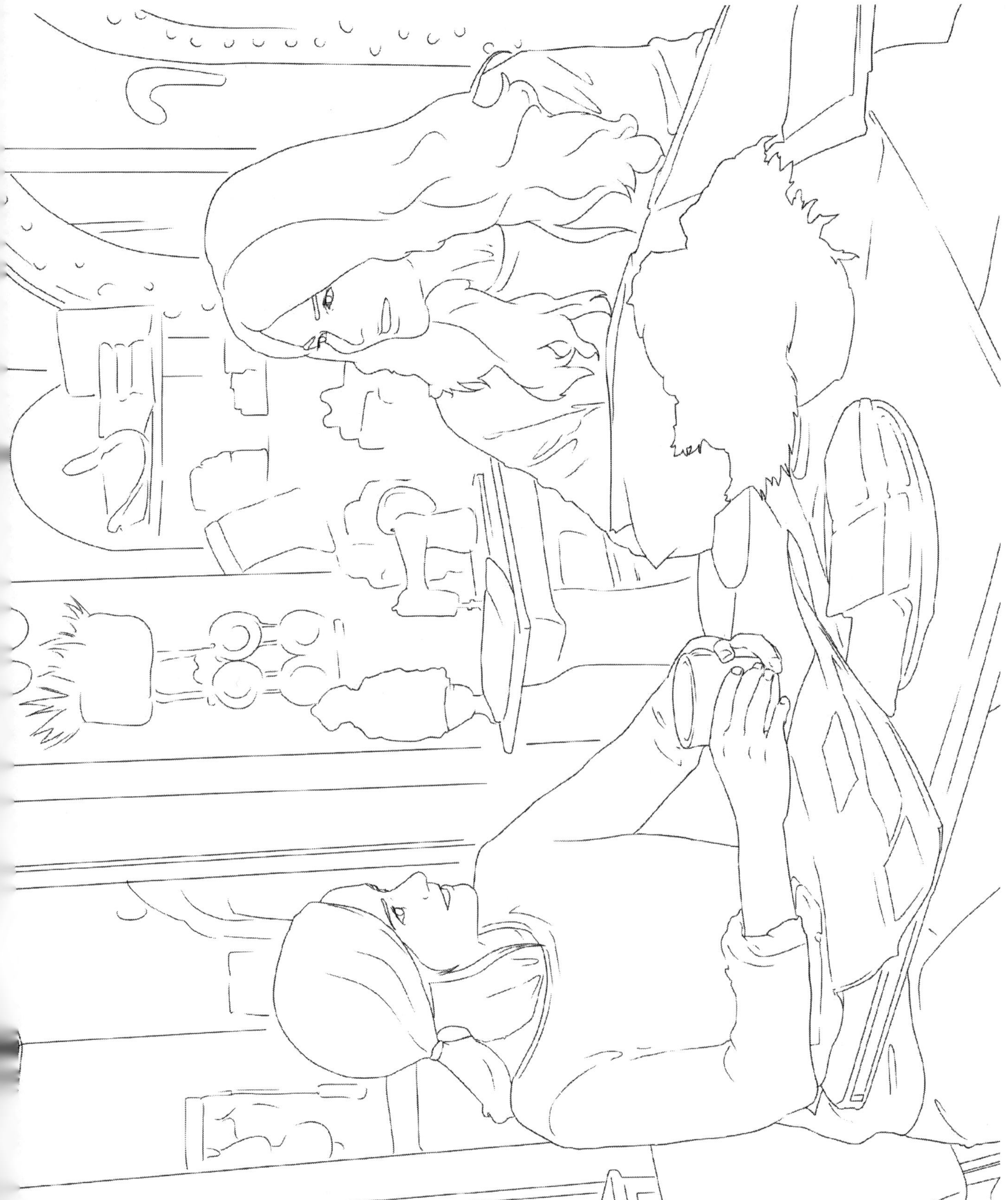

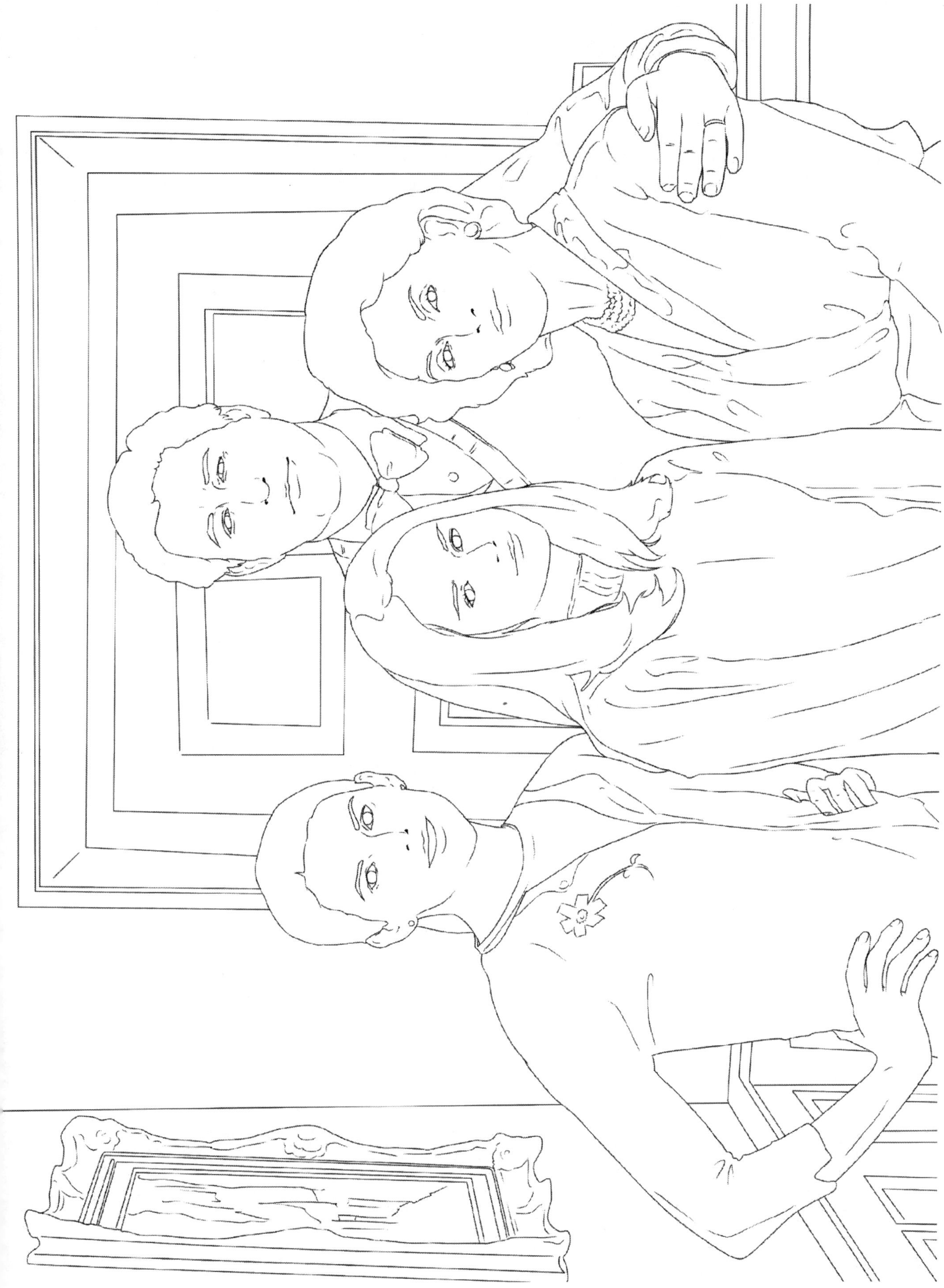

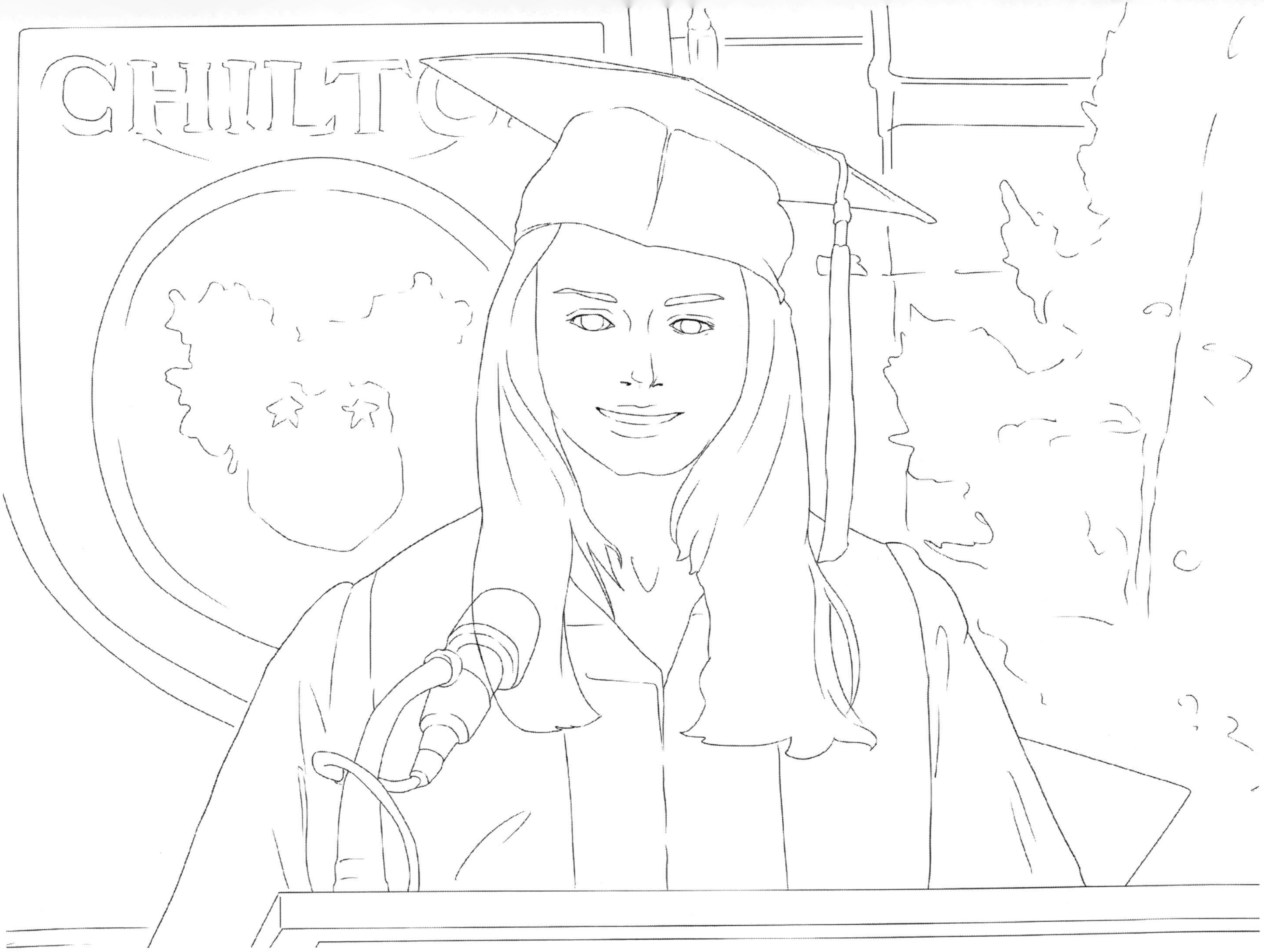
CHILT

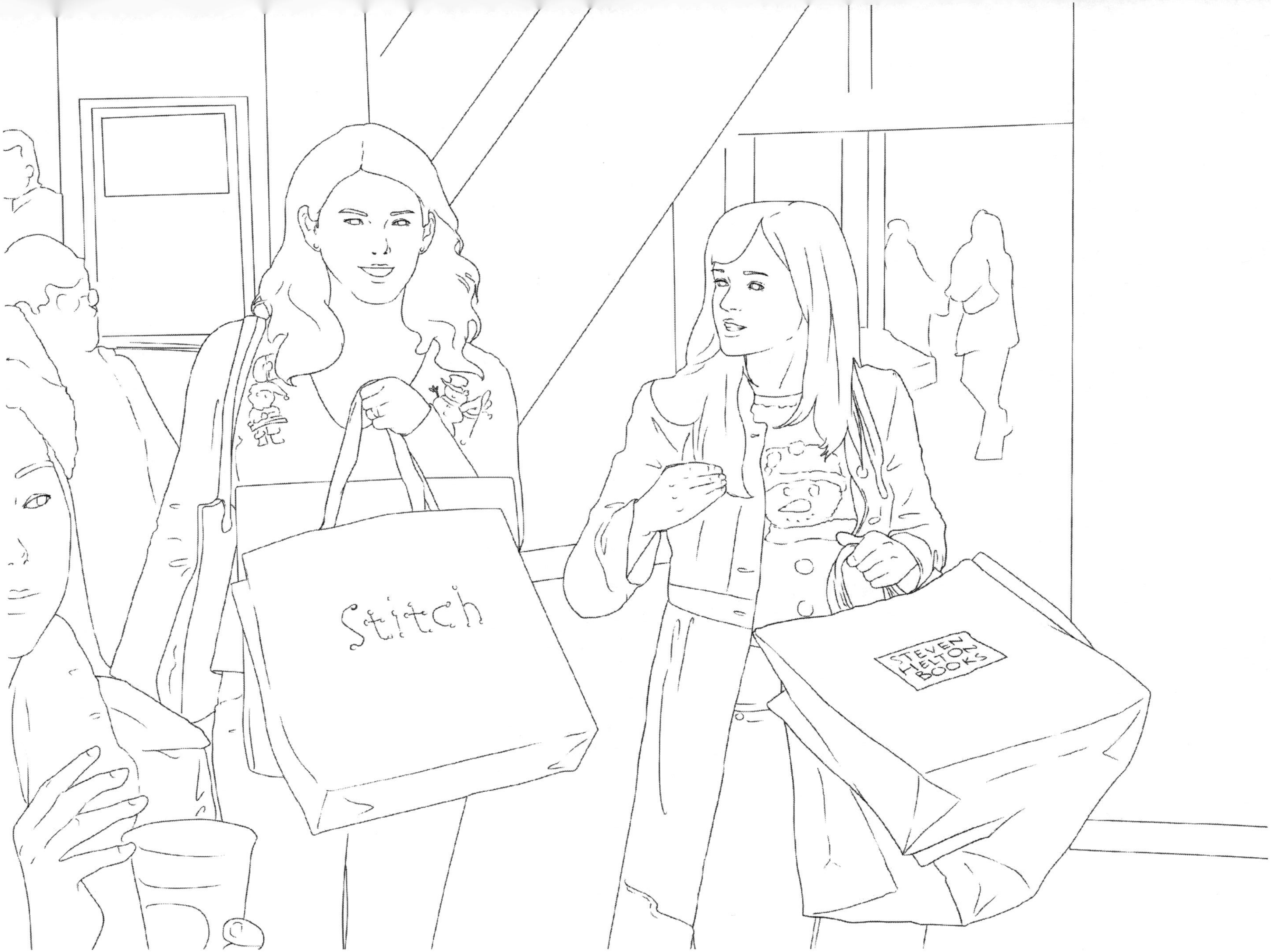

Stitch
STEVEN HELTON BOOKS

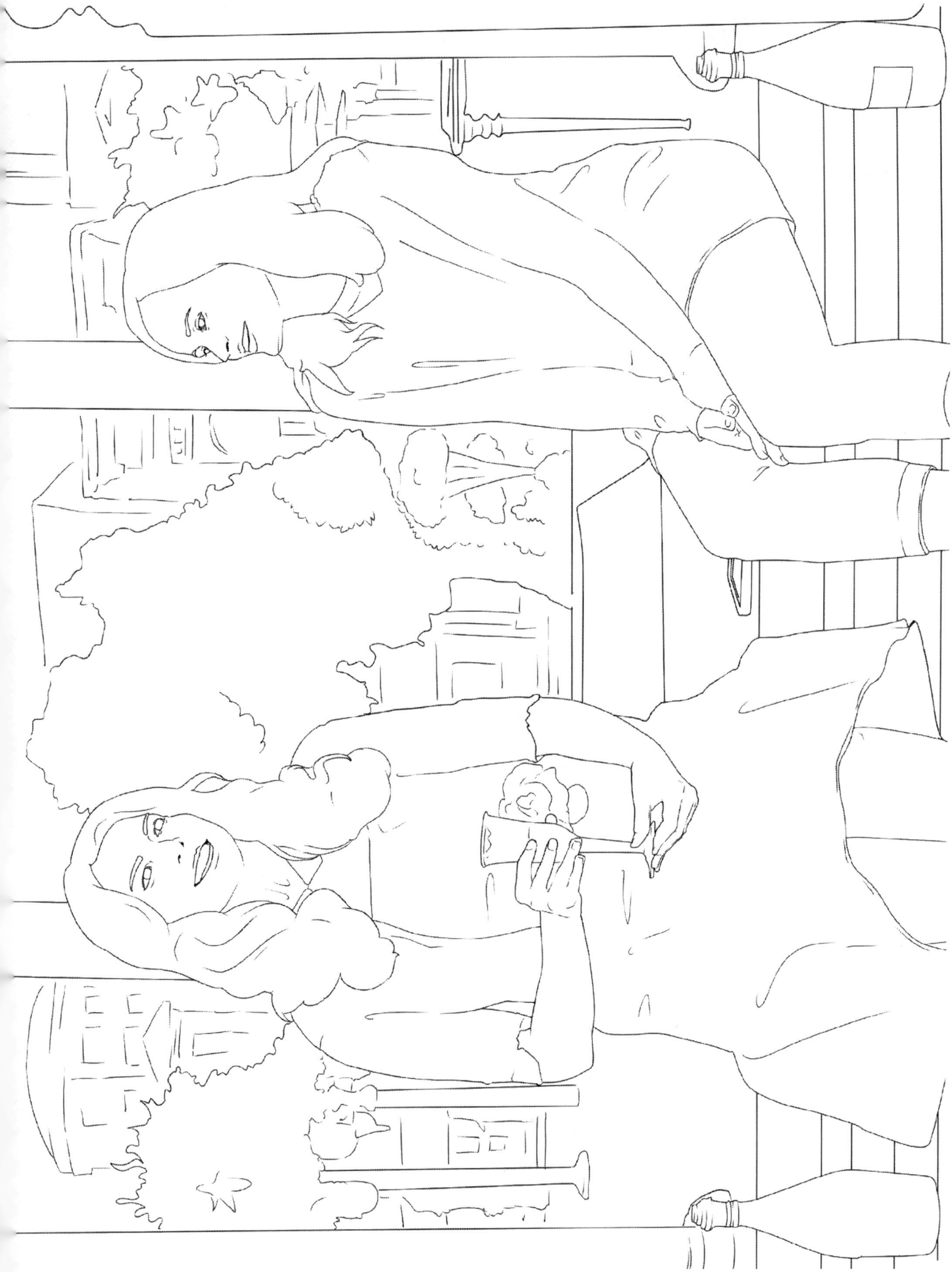

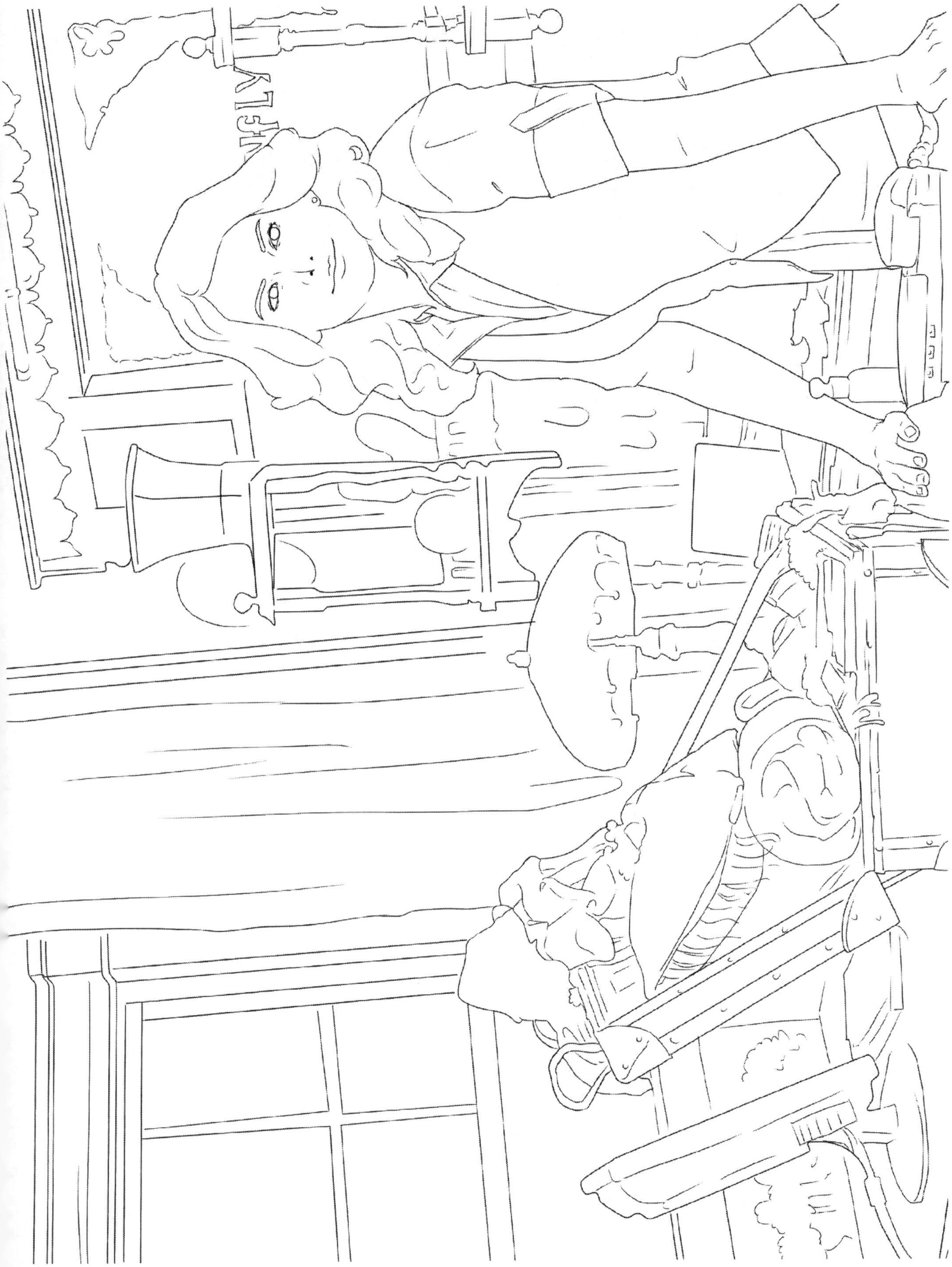

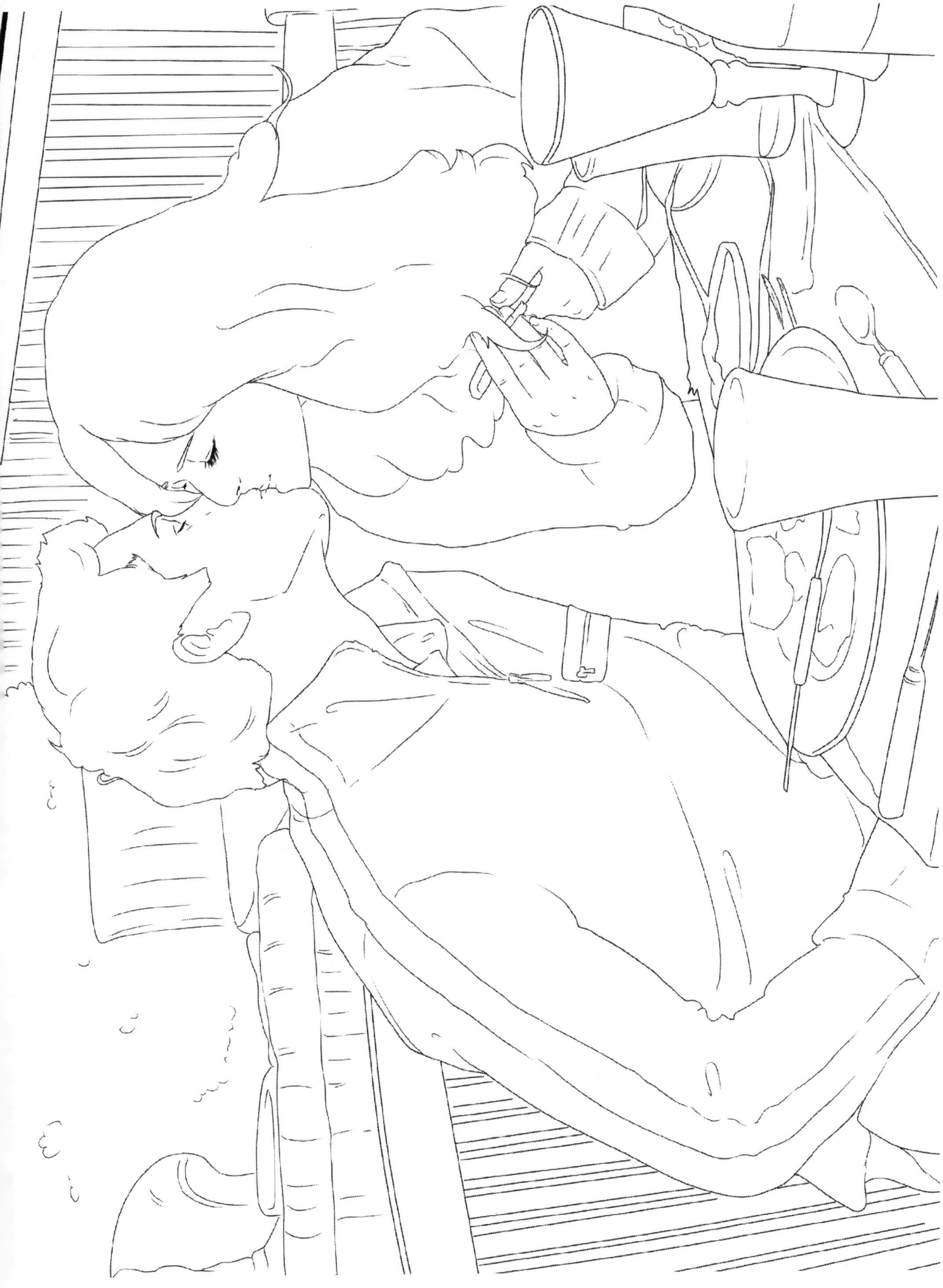

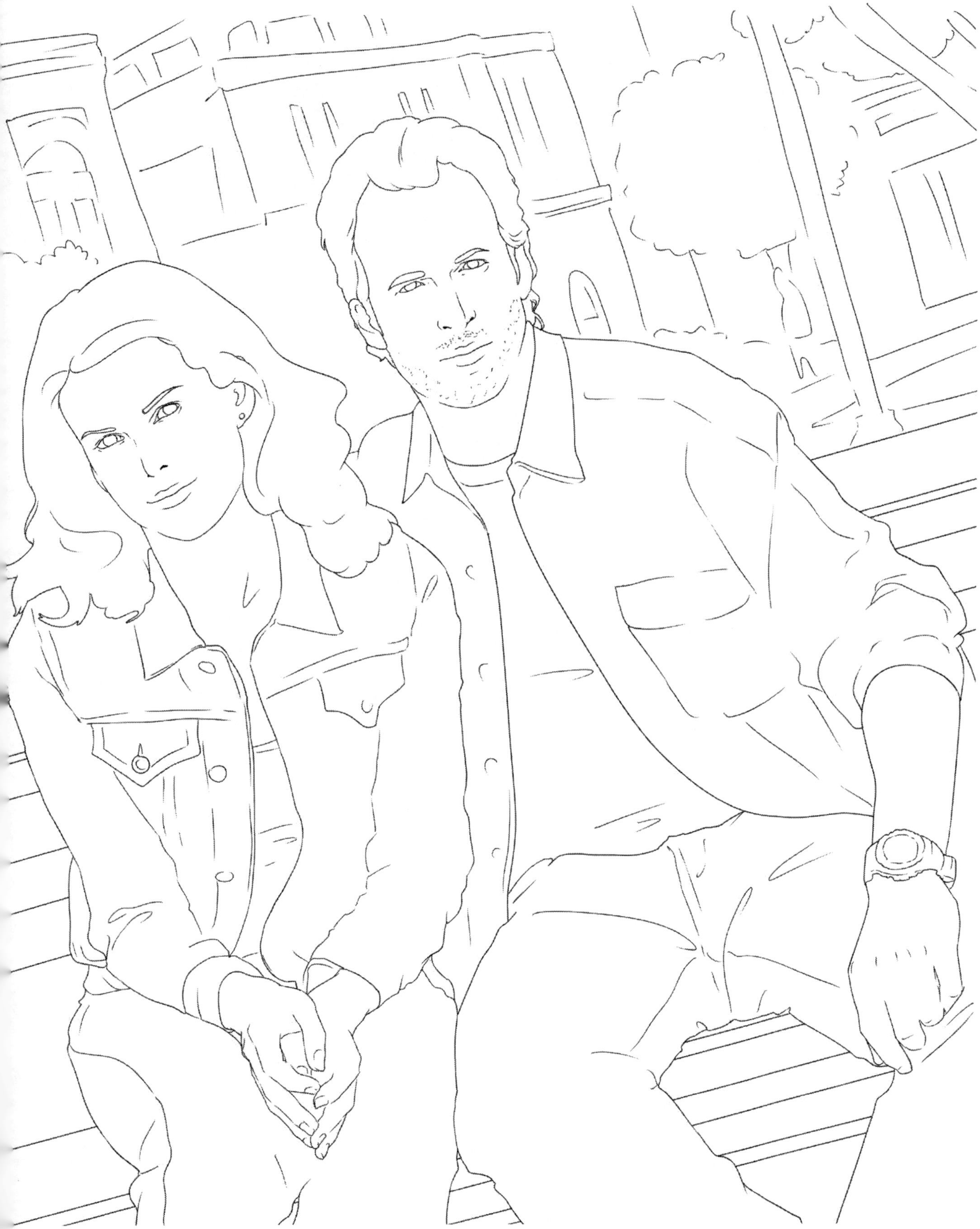

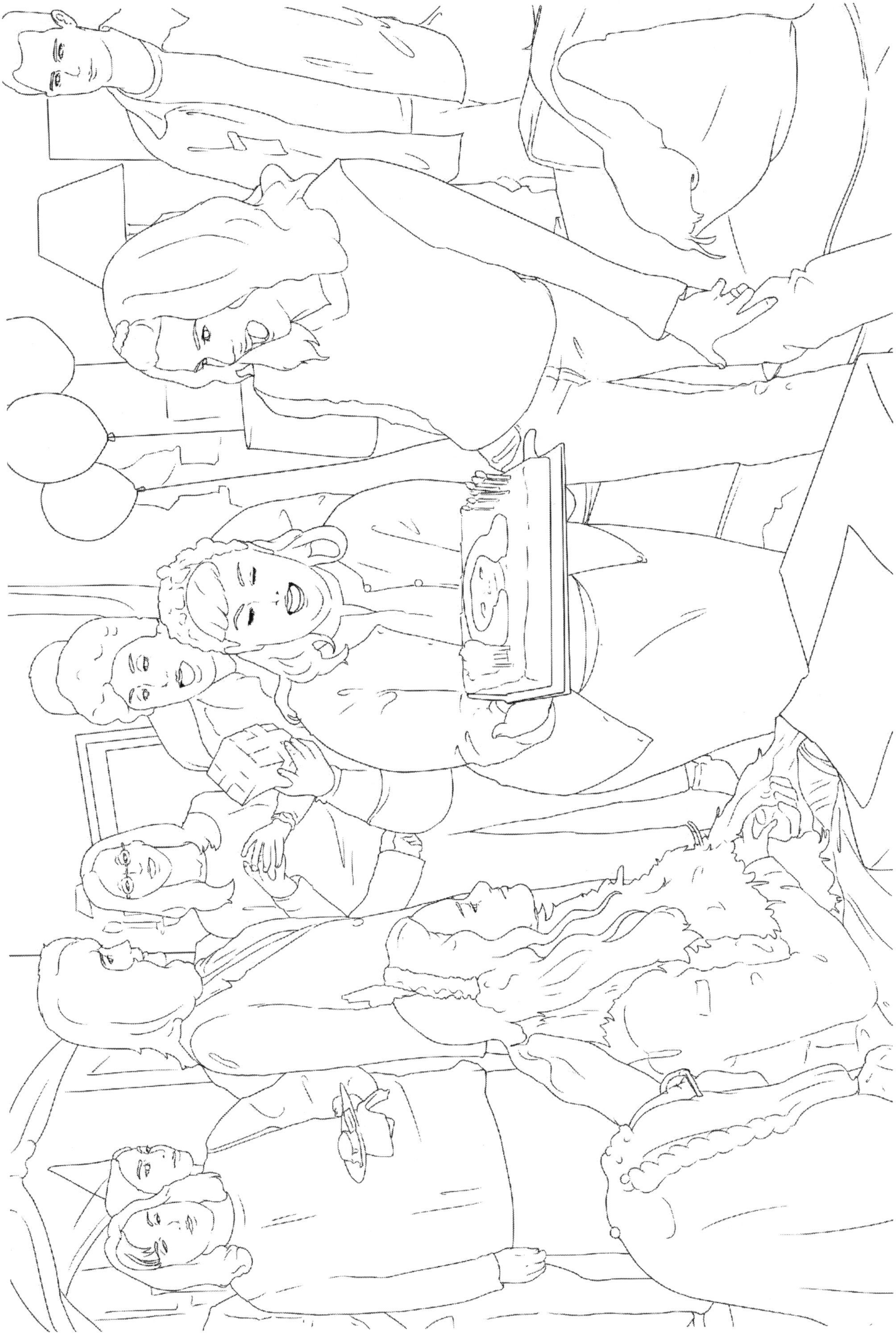

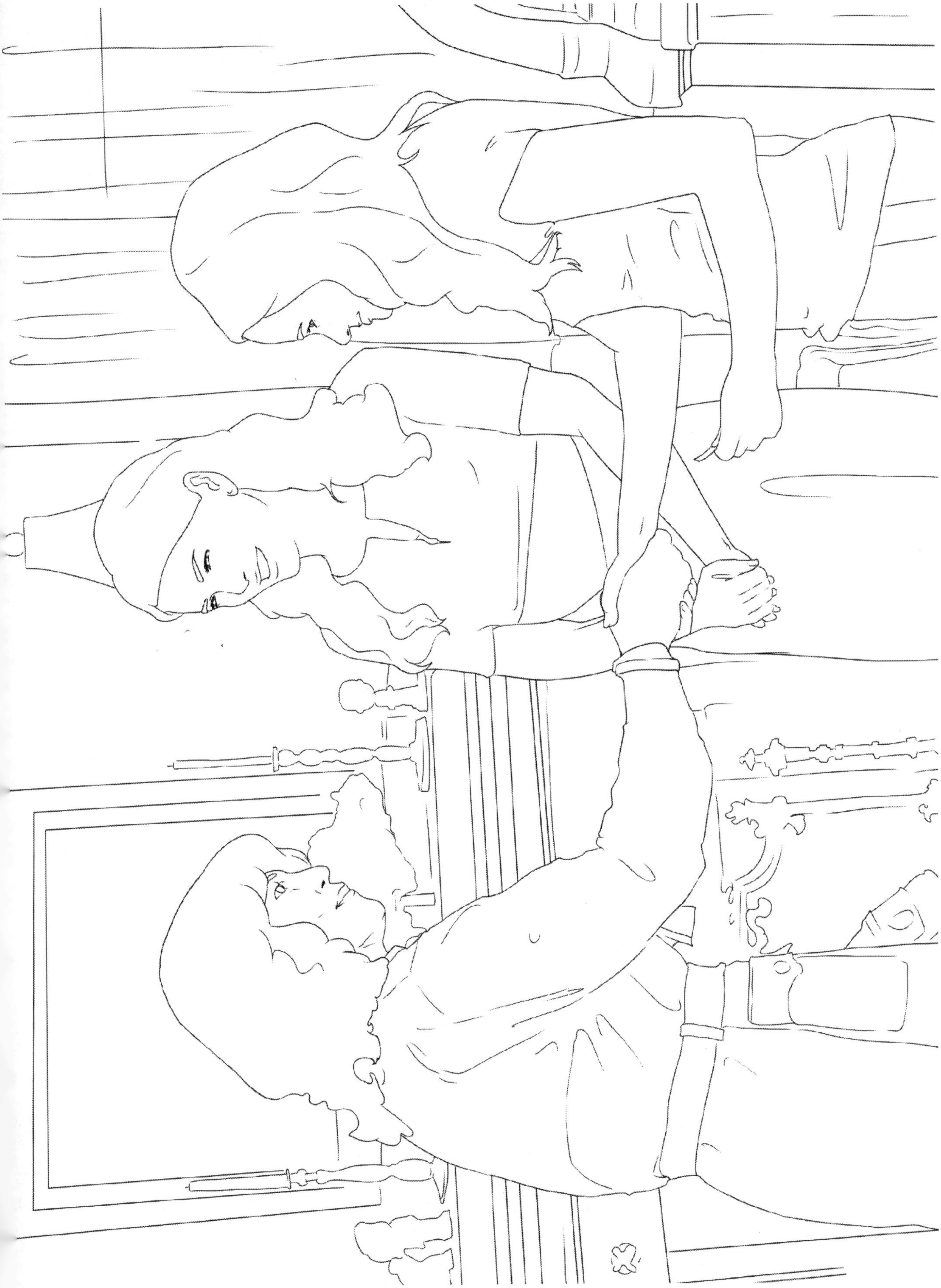

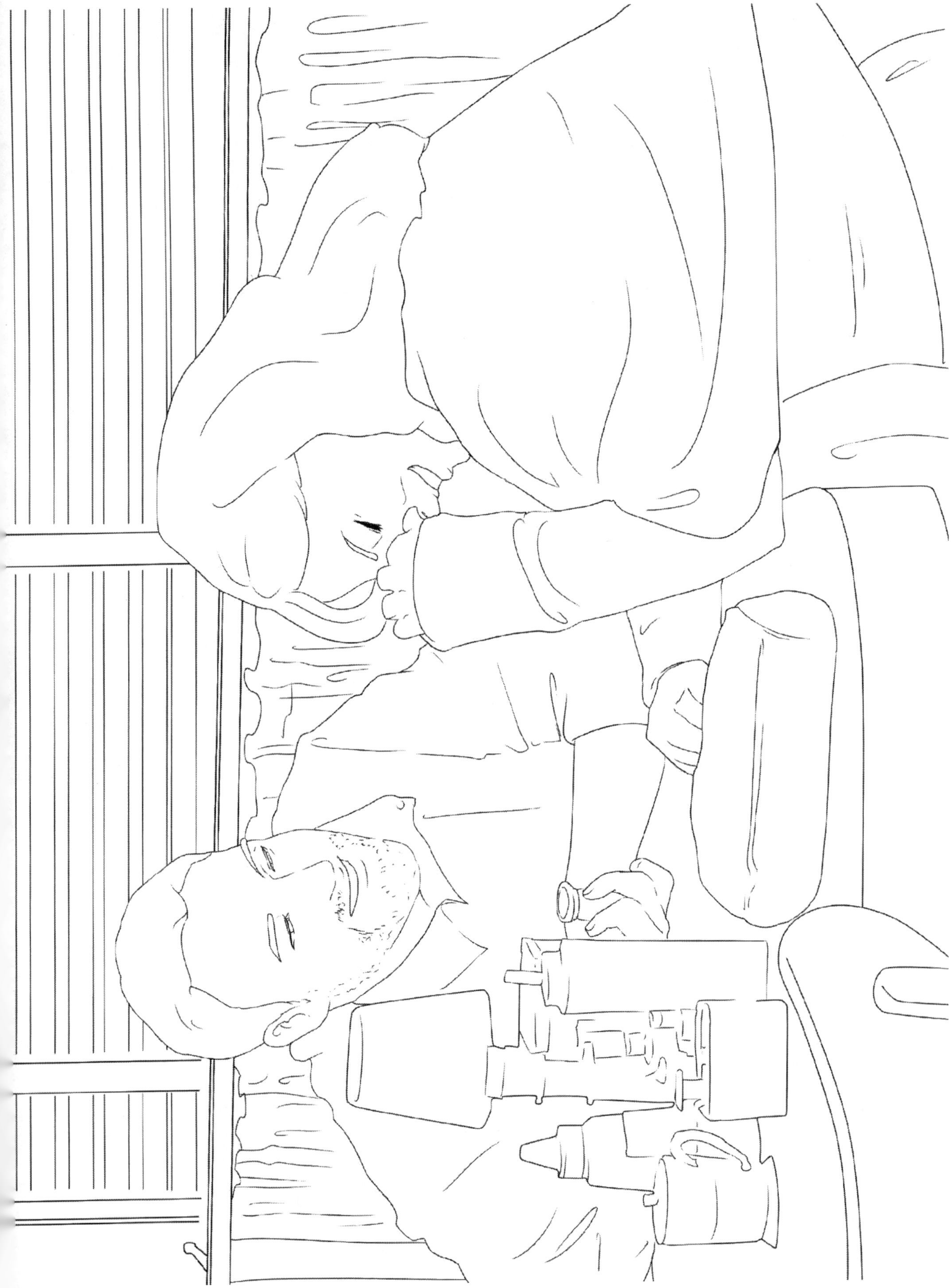

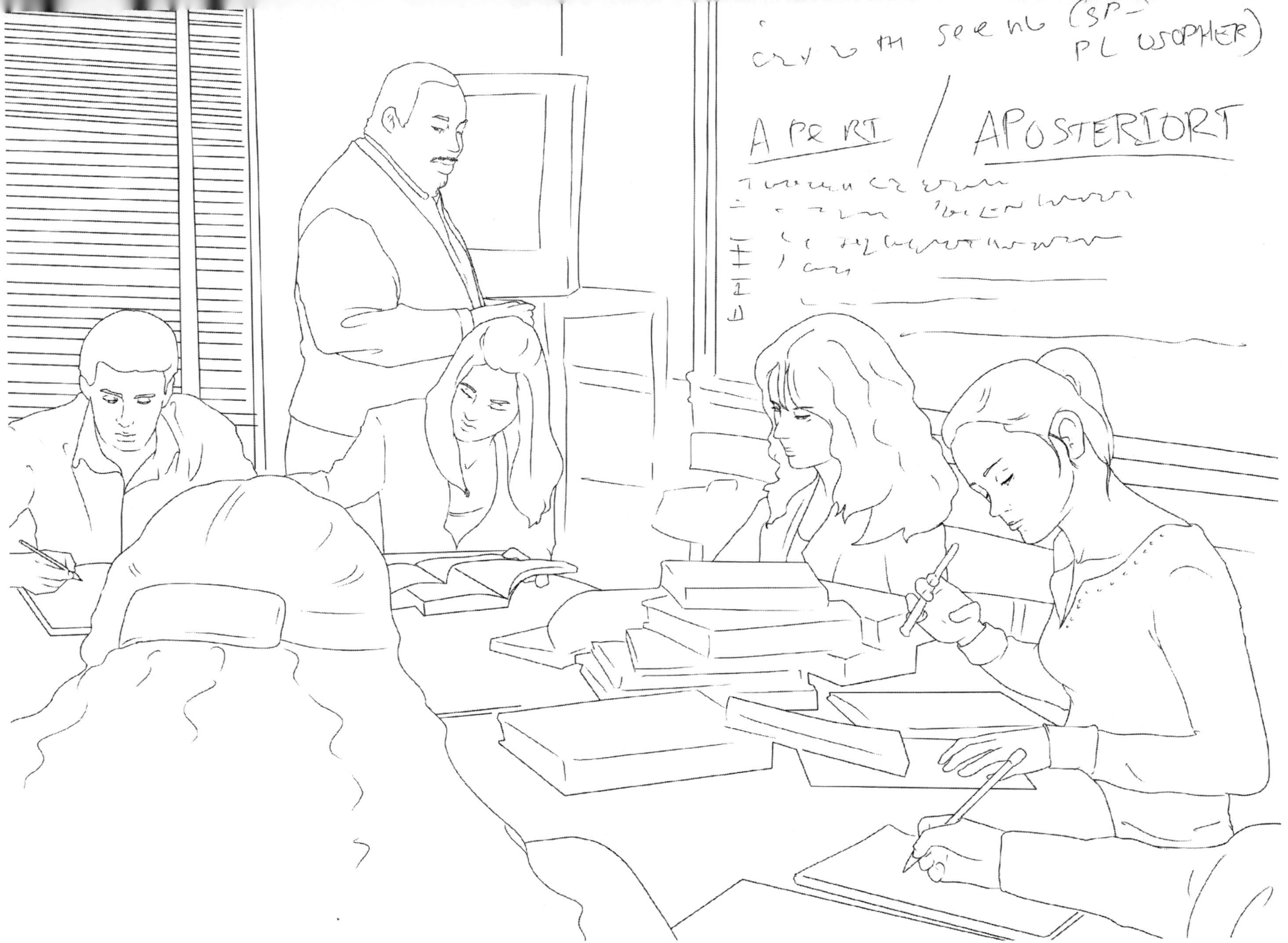
APOSTERIORI

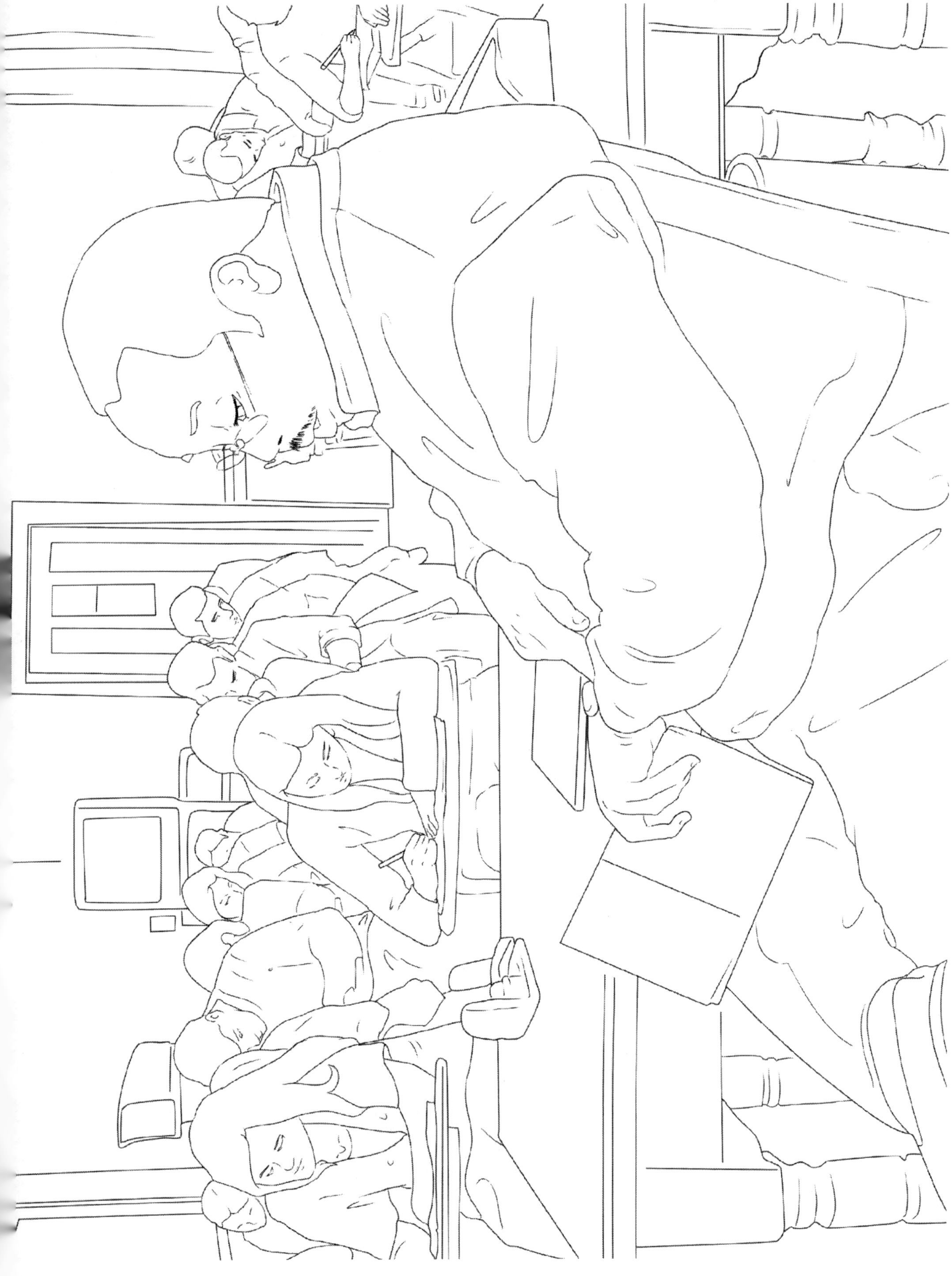

62194059R00035

Made in the USA
Middletown, DE
19 January 2018